CONTENTS

- Transitioning BDRs to AEs, RevOps, and Beyond
- Tailoring Development Plans to Individual Strengths
- The Role of Mentorship and Coaching

- **Chapter 7: Transition Planning**..(92-102)
  - Promoting from Within: The Do's and Don'ts
  - Succession Planning for Critical Roles
  - Managing Knowledge Transfer Effectively
  - Resilience in Action: What to Do When the Unexpected Happens

- **Chapter 8: Frameworks and Processes**...(103-116)
  - Developing a Scalable Playbook
  - Integrating Technology into Your Workflow
  - Automating for Efficiency Without Losing the Human Touch
  - Ensuring Data Quality and Analytics

- **Chapter 9: Leadership Best Practices**..(117-127)
  - Coaching: When to Nudge, When to Push
  - Building Trust and Accountability
  - Communication Skills That Inspire Action
  - Dealing with Conflicts Like a Pro
  - Handling Challenges with Grace (or at Least Humor)

- **Chapter 10: Measuring Success**..(128-141)
  - Leading vs. Lagging Indicators
  - Reviewing Team and Individual Performance
  - Using Feedback Loops for Continuous Improvement
  - Iterating on Strategies That Work

- **Chapter 11: Rethinking Frameworks**...(142-154)
  - Common Qualification Frameworks: Why They're Outdated
  - Introducing the IMPACT Framework for Qualification
  - Limitations of the IMPACT Framework
  - How IMPACT Makes Qualification Smarter and More Effective

Chapter 0: C.R.A.F.T.

What is the CRAFT Framework?

The CRAFT Framework is my leadership and operational philosophy, purpose-built to address the unique challenges of running and scaling a BDR team. It's a holistic system designed to empower sales teams with a balance of innovation, structure, personal growth, and data-driven accountability.

Scaling a BDR function requires more than just adding headcount—it demands a culture and operational backbone that can sustain high performance at scale. Without such a system, teams risk falling into chaos, inefficiency, and burnout. The CRAFT Framework is the antidote, aligning creativity and repeatability with skill-building and accountability to create a BDR operation that grows with your business.

Here's a detailed breakdown of the framework and why it's crucial for scaling a BDR function:

C - Creativity: Innovating to Break Through
- **Why It Matters for Scaling:** As a team grows, creativity ensures that the outreach doesn't become stale or robotic. Larger teams mean more voices reaching out to prospects, and creativity helps maintain individuality and personalization, even in scaled operations.
- **How It Enables Scaling:** By embedding a culture of innovation, creativity prevents a "cookie-cutter" approach that prospects can spot (and ignore) from a mile away. Creative approaches become the differentiator, even as outreach volumes grow.

R - Repeatability: Establishing Scalable Systems
- **Why It Matters for Scaling:** Repeatable processes are the backbone of any scalable BDR operation. Without them, what works for 5 reps can't work for 50, and inconsistency creeps in.
- **How It Enables Scaling:** Repeatability allows new hires to ramp quickly, ensures consistency in quality and messaging, and reduces inefficiencies that arise as the team expands. Playbooks, workflows, and templates create a shared operational language across the team.
- *Example: A shared outreach cadence for enterprise accounts ensures everyone on the team follows proven steps to engage high-value prospects effectively.*

A - Accountability: Creating Ownership at Every Level
- **Why It Matters for Scaling:** As teams grow, individual accountability prevents a "tragedy of the commons" scenario, where the absence of personal ownership leads to declining performance. Scaling without accountability creates blind spots in performance and makes leadership overly reliant on constant oversight.

ACKNOWLEDGEMENTS

To the prospects who slammed the phone on me—you were my first, albeit unwilling, teachers. Every abrupt "Not interested" and glorious hang-up sharpened my resilience and taught me that awkward silence is a powerful motivator. Honestly, you built the foundation of my sales career, so... thanks, I guess?

To the companies that taught me how to run a business—you're the true architects of this book. Your focus, strategy, and occasional brilliance made everything seem possible.

And to the companies that taught me how not to run a business—oh boy, where do I begin? Your commitment to chaos, mismanagement, and "leadership" that felt more like watching a train wreck in slow motion was a sight to behold. You taught me everything NOT to do, and for that, I begrudgingly thank you. Your legacy lives on in this book as a shining example of what to avoid at all costs.

To my wife, who still hasn't left me after countless dinner-table rants about quota resets, pipeline strategies, and "that one meeting that could've been an email"—your endurance deserves a standing ovation. Honestly, your patience is the stuff of legends (and probably needs its own handbook).

To the team members who challenged me, resisted me, and made me fight for every ounce of progress—you kept me sharp, made me better, and occasionally made me want to throw my laptop out the window. You were right more often than I'd like to admit, but don't get used to hearing that.

To the managers who trusted me—you were brave, probably a little reckless, and somehow decided to take a chance on me. And to the ones who couldn't stand me—thank you for the sleepless nights and for being the unwitting inspiration behind many of my successes. You may not have liked me, but you sure made me better.

Finally, to the world of sales—the cold calls, the CRM crashes, the impossible quotas, and the never-ending hustle—you've been both my greatest challenge and my greatest teacher. This book exists because of you, and because therapy isn't always covered by insurance.

Here's to the madness, the lessons, and the scars that turned into stories.

Cheers!

HOW TO USE THIS BOOK

This book isn't just a guide—it's your survival kit for leading a BDR team without losing your sanity (or your job). Whether you're stepping into leadership for the first time or you've been managing BDRs longer than CRM glitches have existed, this book will meet you where you are.

Here's how you can make the most of it:

Skip Around, If You Want
Leadership isn't linear, and neither is this book. Dive into the sections you need most—whether it's setting targets, motivating your team, or fixing a process that's more broken than a Monday morning coffee machine.

Bookmark the Tools and Frameworks
Throughout the book, you'll find practical tools, scorecards, and real-world examples that you can steal—er, implement—immediately. These are designed to make your life easier and your team more successful.

Laugh a Little, Learn a Lot
This isn't a dry textbook. Expect a few laughs, a dose of sarcasm, and the occasional brutally honest truth about what it takes to build a world-class BDR team.

Survive Gen Z (Barely)
Let's be real—leading a team full of Gen Z BDRs is like herding cats, except the cats are multitasking on Slack, TikTok, and their side hustles. Don't worry; this book has tips for handling their unique brand of brilliance and, yes, occasional shithosery.

Use It as a Reality Check
Think your team's struggles are unique? Spoiler: they're not. This book will help you diagnose problems, create solutions, and maybe even make peace with the chaos.

Come Back to It Often
Leadership isn't one-and-done. Whether you're onboarding new BDRs, rethinking KPIs, or planning your team's next big win, this book will be here waiting for you. Dog-ear the pages, write in the margins, and let it grow with you.

Most importantly, remember that leading a BDR team is as much about growth and grit as it is about strategy and structure. Let this book be your partner in crime—or at least the thing you reach for when you're ready to scream into a pillow.

WHY THIS BOOK EXISTS

This is not the kind of handbook you'd willingly pick up if you knew what was in store for you as a BDR leader. But here you are, probably questioning your life choices while trying to figure out why running a BDR team feels like conducting an orchestra of cats with attitude problems.

BDR leadership is a world of glorious chaos. Your job isn't just to lead—it's to untangle messes, inspire creativity, and somehow make hitting quota seem like an achievable goal instead of an elaborate prank. You're managing a team that balances on the fine line between brilliance and baffling decisions ("No, calling the CFO at midnight isn't 'bold,' it's insane.").

This book doesn't exist to stroke your ego or bore you with corporate buzzwords. It's here to hold your hand—or shove you forward, depending on the day—and guide you through the trenches of BDR leadership. Consider it part battle plan, part therapy session, and part intervention for all the times you thought, "Maybe we don't actually need a process."

What Makes This Book Worth Reading?
This book won't tell you to "inspire your team" or "lead with empathy." You already know that (and if you don't, maybe Google it). Instead, it's packed with:
- **Practical tactics** for solving real problems, like why your team still thinks LinkedIn requests count as outreach.
- **Brutally honest** insights about why some teams thrive while others implode spectacularly.
- **Unfiltered humor** to remind you that it's okay to laugh at the absurdity of managing people who once tried to send a breakup email to a prospect.

This isn't about making you feel warm and fuzzy; it's about giving you the tools to survive and thrive in a role where the unexpected is your daily routine.

Why Leading BDRs is Like Surviving Reality TV
If being a sales manager is tough, leading BDRs is like getting dropped into a survival show where the rules change every five minutes, and the contestants (your team) keep eating the strategy playbook. Your role is to build a team that doesn't just hit numbers but evolves into a powerhouse of creativity, resilience, and occasionally good decision-making.

Done right, your BDR team becomes the engine of the company, driving pipeline, revenue, and growth. Done wrong? Well, let's just say you'll end up starring in a cautionary tale about why leadership isn't for everyone.

So, here's the deal: This book won't solve all your problems, but it will give you the tools, perspective, and possibly the sense of humor you'll need to tackle them head-on.

Let's get into it.

CONTENTS

- **Chapter 0: C.R.A.F.T** ....(1-6)
    - What is CRAFT Framework?
    - Why is it relevant to BDR world
    - Simplest ways to implement it
    - Why it works?

- **Chapter 1: Setting Up a BDR Team** ....(7-24)
    - Defining the BDR Role
    - Recruitment Strategies
    - Crafting Effective Job Descriptions
    - The 30, 60, 90-Day Onboarding Plan
    - Essential Tools and Resources
    - Setting Early Expectations

- **Chapter 2: Setting Targets and KPIs** ....(25-39)
    - The Science Behind Why Targets and KPIs Work
    - Activity vs. Outcome Metrics
    - The Art and Science of Quotas
    - Balancing Individual and Team Success
    - Encouraging Collaboration While Maintaining Accountability
    - Adjusting Targets for Changing Realities

- **Chapter 3: Headcount Planning** ....(40-53)
    - Determining Team Size and Structure
    - The Ideal Manager-to-Rep Ratio
    - BDR-to-AE Ratios That Work
    - Scaling for Growth (and Surviving It)
    - Seasonal vs. Long-Term Needs
    - Budgeting for Team Expansion

- **Chapter 4: What to Expect of BDRs (Daily, Weekly, Monthly)** ....(54-66)
    - A Day in the Life of a BDR
    - Weekly Routines for Success
    - Mastering the Monthly Rhythm
    - Creating Consistency Without Micromanaging

- **Chapter 5: Motivating Your BDR Team** ....(67-80)
    - Aligning Professional Goals with Personal Dreams
    - Incentive Programs That Actually Work
    - Recognizing and Celebrating Successes
    - Avoiding Burnout in a High-Pressure Role
    - Team Book Reading, Mock Calls, and Call-Listening Sessions

- **Chapter 6: Career Planning for BDRs** ....(81-91)
    - Building a Career Path That Retains Talent

Chapter 0: C.R.A.F.T.

- **How It Enables Scaling:** When reps take ownership of their performance, managers can focus on strategic initiatives rather than micromanaging. Accountability becomes a self-reinforcing system that supports autonomy and innovation while maintaining high standards.

F - Focus on Skill Development: Building a Sustainable Talent Pipeline
- **Why It Matters for Scaling:** Scaling a BDR function isn't just about hiring—it's about growing your existing talent. Skill development ensures that your team evolves alongside the increasing complexity of your operation, reducing turnover and creating a pipeline of leaders who can take on more responsibility.
- **How It Enables Scaling:** Regular training and coaching sessions embed adaptability into your team, preparing them to tackle new challenges as the business grows. A team that continuously develops its skills will consistently exceed expectations and adapt to changing market dynamics.

T - Transparency through Data: Driving Decision-Making with Insights
- **Why It Matters for Scaling:** Scaling a team without data transparency is like driving a car without a dashboard. It becomes impossible to identify bottlenecks, replicate successes, or make informed decisions as the operation grows.
- **How It Enables Scaling:** Shared dashboards, team-wide performance reviews, and real-time insights create a feedback loop that ensures alignment and continuous improvement, even as the team scales. Data empowers leaders to identify underperforming areas and celebrate what's working at scale.

Why Scaling a BDR Function Is Crucial

The BDR team is the frontline engine that drives your company's pipeline. A well-scaled BDR function ensures:

- **Predictable Growth:** By systematizing pipeline generation, you create a steady stream of opportunities that fuel revenue growth.
- **Resilience Against Market Changes:** A scalable BDR team can adapt to shifts in market conditions, ensuring continued pipeline generation even during downturns.
- **Talent Development for the Organization:** Scaling a BDR function isn't just about the immediate pipeline—it's about creating a talent pipeline for your sales and leadership teams. A well-developed BDR program feeds AEs, RevOps, and even future managers.
- **Operational Efficiency:** Scaling creates economies of scale, where repeatable processes and shared resources drive down the cost of pipeline generation per rep.

Without a framework like CRAFT, scaling often leads to diminishing returns, inconsistent performance, and high turnover. By embedding CRAFT principles, you ensure that growth isn't just bigger but also better.

What is CRAFT Framework?

Chapter 0: C.R.A.F.T.

Why is the CRAFT Framework Relevant to the BDR World?

The BDR role is dynamic and ever-evolving, requiring a blend of strategic creativity, consistent execution, and adaptability. Scaling a BDR function only amplifies these demands. To navigate this landscape, the CRAFT Framework offers a structured yet flexible approach, grounded in principles that resonate with real-world challenges.

Real-World Scenarios That Show the Power of CRAFT
Breaking Through Market Noise

Picture this: Your BDRs are targeting time-strapped CTOs at scaling startups. Their inboxes are flooded with sales emails daily, and your team's efforts are lost in the mix. A junior rep experiments with a fresh idea—creating a 30-second video personalized to the CTO's LinkedIn activity, referencing a post about their recent cloud migration. The message lands, earning a response and sparking a meaningful conversation.

This isn't luck; it's creativity with intent—a hallmark of the CRAFT Framework.

From Chaos to Consistency During Rapid Growth

Your BDR team grows from 5 to 20 in under six months. With this growth comes the inevitable chaos—mixed messaging, inconsistent processes, and uneven results. By introducing structured workflows and shared outreach cadences, your team stabilizes. New hires ramp faster, veteran reps perform more efficiently, and the team delivers consistent results, quarter after quarter.

When Resilience is Tested

It's Q4, and rejection rates are at an all-time high due to tightened budgets. The team's morale is sinking, and so are their results. Instead of focusing solely on quotas, you schedule weekly call-listening sessions to identify patterns, coach on objection handling, and celebrate incremental wins. The shift in focus revitalizes the team's energy, improving their meeting booking rate by 15% within weeks.

Tackling a New Market

Your company pivots to targeting enterprise accounts, a space with complex buying cycles and multi-threaded decision-making. The shift feels daunting, but with focused training on executive-level messaging and tools that track stakeholder engagement, your team adapts. Within three months, they're booking meetings with 25% of target accounts—opening doors to larger opportunities.

Retaining Rising Stars

One of your top-performing BDRs, frustrated by a lack of growth opportunities, is considering a move. Instead of losing them, you implement a personalized development plan, showing a clear path to becoming an Account Executive within

Chapter 0: C.R.A.F.T.

the next 12 months. They stay, motivated not just by immediate success but by the promise of a career.

These scenarios illustrate the transformative potential of a well-executed BDR function. With the CRAFT Framework as your guide, your team isn't just surviving —it's thriving.

Simplest Ways to Implement the CRAFT Framework

The CRAFT Framework may sound comprehensive, but implementing it doesn't have to be daunting. In fact, its strength lies in how seamlessly it integrates into the day-to-day operations of a BDR team. Whether you're starting from scratch or refining an existing team, here's how to bring each pillar to life in practical, straightforward ways:

C - Creativity: Foster Innovation in Outreach
- **Weekly Idea Sprints:** Dedicate 15 minutes in team meetings to brainstorm unconventional outreach ideas.
  - *Example: "What's a unique way to engage a prospect who hasn't responded to traditional emails?"*
- **Content Libraries:** Provide BDRs with ready-to-use assets like videos, infographics, and case studies that they can customize for outreach.
- **Freedom to Experiment:** Allocate 10% of their prospecting time to try new tactics. For instance:
  - Sending a video message through LinkedIn.
  - Writing humorous subject lines to test response rates.

R - Repeatability: Build Scalable Processes
- **Document Everything:** Create a centralized playbook with outreach cadences, email templates, and qualification frameworks.
  - Tip: Update the playbook quarterly based on performance insights.
- **Standardize Onboarding:** Use structured 30-60-90 day plans to ensure every new BDR ramps up quickly and consistently.
- **Automate Where Possible:**
  - Use sales engagement platforms like Outreach.io to automate cadences.
  - Set reminders for follow-ups to reduce mental load on reps.

A - Accountability: Make Ownership a Team Value
- **Daily Stand-Ups:** Have BDRs share their top goals for the day. End with quick updates on progress to foster accountability.
- **Shared Dashboards:** Use a tool like Salesforce to maintain visibility into team performance metrics. When everyone sees the same data, it encourages accountability without micromanagement.
- **Feedback Loops:** Regular one-on-ones focus on reflecting on performance, celebrating wins, and addressing challenges.

Chapter 0: C.R.A.F.T.

F - Focus on Skill Development: Prioritize Growth
- **Role-Playing Sessions:** Weekly role-plays that mimic real-world scenarios (e.g., handling objections or pitching to a skeptical CFO).
    - Tip: Rotate leadership for these sessions, letting senior reps coach junior ones.
- **Learning Time:** Dedicate 1 hour per week for BDRs to explore industry trends, tools, or sales tactics. Provide access to learning platforms like LinkedIn Learning or Gong Academy.
- **Progression Plans:** Share clear career paths with milestones for transitioning to roles like AE or RevOps.

T - Transparency through Data: Create Clarity and Trust
- **Performance Dashboards:** Use live dashboards to track metrics like meetings booked, response rates, and pipeline value.
    - Tip: Keep the focus on trends and insights, not just numbers.
- **Open Reviews:** Share what's working (and what's not) in team meetings, encouraging collaboration and continuous improvement.
- **Win Stories:** Highlight successful outreach examples from the team, explaining what made them work.

Quick Wins to Start Today

- **Day 1:** Implement daily stand-ups to set clear goals and establish accountability.
- **Week 1:** Schedule a brainstorming session for creative outreach ideas and document the top three tactics to test.
- **Month 1:** Roll out a shared performance dashboard and a structured 30-60-90 day onboarding plan.
- **Quarter 1:** Launch a team playbook with repeatable processes and review it quarterly.

By starting small and layering in these practices, you can quickly establish the CRAFT Framework as the foundation of your BDR team's culture and operations.

Why the CRAFT Framework Works

The CRAFT Framework works because it addresses the critical needs of a BDR team: creativity, consistency, accountability, skill development, and data-driven decision-making. Here's why these principles drive success:

Balances Creativity and Process
BDRs need both innovative outreach tactics and repeatable workflows. The CRAFT Framework harmonizes these elements, enabling teams to scale without losing the personal touch.

Chapter 0: C.R.A.F.T.

Builds a Culture of Ownership
Teams thrive when individuals feel accountable for their outcomes. CRAFT empowers reps to take control of their performance metrics.
- In a study by Gallup, organizations with higher employee accountability report 22% greater profitability. For instance, a BDR analyzing their own drop in call-to-meeting conversion rates adjusts their pitch and sees a 10% improvement in two weeks.

Promotes Scalable Success
Without repeatable systems, scaling a BDR team leads to inefficiencies and performance inconsistencies. CRAFT ensures that processes remain effective, even as the team grows.
- Data shows that companies with standardized sales processes see 33% higher revenue growth compared to those without. A team adopting structured onboarding cuts ramp time for new hires by 30%, improving pipeline contributions sooner.

Encourages Continuous Improvement
By integrating skill development and transparent performance reviews, CRAFT fosters an iterative culture of learning and growth.
- According to Gong.io, reps who receive weekly feedback improve their call effectiveness by 19% over three months. A team identifies that video prospecting yields 20% higher response rates and incorporates it into their standard training.

Supports Team Resilience
High-pressure roles like BDRs need a framework that mitigates burnout and keeps morale high. CRAFT emphasizes support through coaching, structured workflows, and clear expectations.
- A survey by McKinsey found that 45% of salespeople cite a lack of support as the primary reason for burnout. By implementing weekly role-plays, a team improves objection handling, boosting meeting booking rates by 15% in one month.

Why the CRAFT Framework Stands Out
- **Psychology-Driven Design:** Aligns with how people work best: clarity reduces stress, accountability drives motivation, and small wins reinforce success.
- **Scalable by Nature:** Processes and data ensure that what works for five reps will work for 50.
- **Proven in Practice:** Whether backed by industry research or real-world outcomes, the principles of CRAFT are rooted in measurable success.

Chapter 1: Setting Up a BDR Team

Building a BDR team is like drafting the opening act for the greatest show your company has ever put on. These are the people who set the stage, draw in the audience, and make sure the main event (your Account Executives) doesn't fall flat. They're the first spark of engagement, the ones who light the fire and pass it on for others to fan into a full blaze.

In many ways, BDRs are as important as CEOs—they're often the first face a prospect sees, the voice that shapes the company's first impression, and the bridge between indifference and interest. No pressure, though.

But let's be clear: creating a powerhouse BDR team doesn't happen by accident. It's not as simple as posting a job ad, hiring someone who "likes people," and throwing them a list of prospects. It takes intention, strategy, and a willingness to think beyond the traditional playbook.

A clear understanding of the role is crucial, but so is the ability to identify unconventional talent and set up systems that equip them for long-term success. A BDR is more than a "junior salesperson"—they're the architects of opportunity, responsible for building the pipeline that keeps your company's revenue engine running.

While it's easy to see the BDR role as entry-level or transactional, it's far more nuanced. These individuals are the first impression of your business—sometimes the only impression a prospect gets before deciding whether to engage further.

It's like being the opening act for a world-famous band: if they fail to captivate, the headliner never gets a chance to shine. When executed well, this role doesn't just drive meetings—it builds trust, uncovers valuable insights, and sets the tone for meaningful relationships.

Defining the BDR Role

Think of a BDR as the face of your company's future revenue. Their role extends far beyond the traditional hustle of dialing numbers and sending emails. BDRs are responsible for sparking meaningful conversations that could lead to business-changing opportunities. In a way, they're like talent scouts—constantly on the lookout for potential stars, except their stars are decision-makers with budget authority.

A great BDR doesn't just regurgitate scripts—they're thoughtful listeners, critical thinkers, and expert researchers. They understand their prospects' industries, challenges, and goals, crafting outreach that speaks directly to those factors. A cold email referencing a prospect's recent blog post or a LinkedIn message highlighting a shared connection signals effort and attention to detail. These seemingly small touches can be the difference between a response and radio silence.

Chapter 1: Setting Up a BDR Team

For example, instead of a generic email like, "*Hi [First Name], we help companies streamline operations,*" a thoughtful BDR might write: "*Hi [First Name], I saw your recent announcement about expanding into Southeast Asia—congratulations! Scaling to new regions can be complex, and our platform helps businesses like yours stay organized during high-growth phases.*"

It's no exaggeration to say that a BDR can make or break a prospect's perception of your company. Imagine the difference between a BDR who treats their role as "just a job" versus one who takes the time to understand a prospect's business challenges, speaks their language, and offers real value. The former leaves prospects indifferent—or worse, annoyed. The latter creates a connection that makes your company stand out in a sea of competitors.

Why Clarity Matters
Defining the BDR role with precision is crucial. Ambiguity leads to confusion, underperformance, and burnout. When responsibilities and expectations are clear—and aligned with broader company goals—BDRs are better equipped to approach their work with confidence and determination.
To drive success, ensure your BDRs understand not just what they need to do but why it matters. This clarity fosters accountability, sharpens their focus, and creates a sense of ownership over their role in the larger sales process.

The Anatomy of a BDR's Day
To succeed, BDRs need to allocate their time effectively. Consider a typical day for a BDR targeting enterprise accounts:

- **70% Researching Decision-Makers:** This involves digging into company structures, identifying key players, and learning about their challenges. Good research isn't just about finding names—it's about context. A BDR who knows a prospect's company is expanding into new markets can tailor their outreach to demonstrate how your product supports that goal.
- **20% Crafting Personalized Outreach:** Personalization is where the magic happens. A well-crafted email or call shows prospects you've done your homework and care about solving their specific problems.
- **10% Updating CRM Data:** Even the best outreach means little if it's not tracked. Keeping the CRM clean ensures continuity, prevents overlap, and enables data-driven decision-making.

Why This Role Matters
When the role is clearly defined and well-supported, a BDR isn't just another cog in the machine. They're the engine of innovation, connection, and growth. A skilled BDR opens doors that would otherwise remain shut, paving the way for AEs to close deals and for your company to achieve its revenue goals.

But let's not sugarcoat it: this role isn't for everyone. It requires resilience, creativity, and a relentless drive to keep going even when the responses are more "no" than

Chapter 1: Setting Up a BDR Team

"yes". That's why it's crucial to hire the right people, set clear expectations, and provide the tools and guidance they need to succeed.

When you do, the results speak for themselves: a thriving pipeline, a stronger sales culture, and a team that's proud of the impact they're making.

Recruitment Strategies: The Art of Finding Unconventional Talent

Hiring BDRs isn't about checking boxes—it's about finding people with the spark to light up a room (or an inbox). Sure, traditional sales experience can help, but some of the best BDRs come from unconventional backgrounds. I've hired former fashion designers, previous founders, and even people who've sold high-end vacuums at Dyson or built sports experiences at Decathlon. What they had in common wasn't their industry experience; it was their curiosity, resilience, and ability to connect with people.

Of course, unconventional talent still needs to align with certain traits to thrive as a BDR. That's where a scorecard comes in. It's a way to evaluate candidates objectively, focusing on what matters most:

Criteria	Description	Rating
Curiosity	Do they ask insightful questions and seek to understand?	
Resilience	Can they handle rejection and bounce back stronger?	
Communication Skills	Do they connect effectively and sound human, not robotic?	
Cultural Fit	Will they thrive in the company's environment?	
Adaptability	Can they roll with changes and thrive in uncertainty?	
Problem-Solving	Do they think critically and offer creative solutions?	

Chapter 1: Setting Up a BDR Team

A hiring scorecard lets you focus on the qualities that matter, not just a shiny resume. Pair this with behavioral interview questions like, "Tell me about a time you convinced someone to change their mind," and you'll spot the stars among the crowd.

To uncover the best candidates, it's essential to move beyond generic questions and dive into scenarios that test how they think, adapt, and problem-solve. Each criterion in the scorecard can be paired with targeted questions that reveal how candidates approach real-world challenges.

Curiosity

Curiosity is the fuel for deeper prospecting and meaningful conversations. You want to find people who are naturally inquisitive, eager to dig deeper, and open to learning.

- Behavioral Question: "Tell me about a time you went out of your way to learn something new that helped you succeed."
- Scenario Question: "You're researching a company with almost no online presence. Their LinkedIn is inactive, and their website is barebones. How would you gather insights to build a compelling outreach?"
- Creative Question: "If you had one question to ask a prospect that would make them talk for 15 minutes straight, what would it be?"

Resilience

Rejection is part of the job, and resilience separates those who keep going from those who fold.

- Behavioral Question: "Describe a time when you faced repeated rejection. How did you stay motivated?"
- Scenario Question: "You've called a prospect six times, and they keep hanging up after two seconds. What's your next move?"
- Creative Question: "If rejection were a person, how would you convince them to give you a chance?"

Communication Skills

Effective communication is clarity, persuasion, and adapting to the listener.

- Behavioral Question: "Give an example of when you had to explain a complex idea to someone unfamiliar with it. How did you ensure they understood?"
- Scenario Question: "Imagine you're tasked with explaining why your product is better than a competitor's to someone who doesn't even know they need it. What would you say?"
- Creative Question: "If emojis were the only language allowed, how would you write a follow-up email to a prospect?"

Cultural Fit

Your team's chemistry matters as much as their skills. You're looking for people who align with your company's values and thrive in the existing team dynamic.

Chapter 1: Setting Up a BDR Team

- Behavioral Question: "What kind of team environment brings out your best work? Describe a time you thrived in that environment."
- Scenario Question: "You're in a team meeting, and someone proposes an idea you strongly disagree with. How do you handle it?"
- Creative Question: "If your workday were a playlist, what three songs would be on it and why?"

Adaptability

The sales world is constantly changing, and adaptability is key to surviving and thriving.

- Behavioral Question: "Tell me about a time you had to change your approach completely because things weren't working. What did you do?"
- Scenario Question: "You're given a new product to sell with minimal training and a short deadline. How would you prepare yourself to pitch it effectively?"
- Creative Question: "If you were thrown into a completely new industry tomorrow, what's the first thing you'd do to get up to speed?"

Problem-Solving

This is where my favorite Bisleri example comes in—testing creativity, analytical thinking, and practical solutions.

- Behavioral Question: "Describe a time when you were faced with a challenging problem and didn't have all the information you needed. How did you approach it?"
- Scenario Question:
- "You're a sales rep for Bisleri, the packaged drinking water company, heading to finalize a deal with a major conglomerate. On your way, you stop at a village with no access to packaged water. Your manager demands you fix this issue immediately. When you speak to the locals, they tell you they fetch water from a well they claim to be the purest in the world. Your challenge is to sell a bottle of water to the well owner. What's your pitch?"
- Creative Question: "If you had to convince someone to buy something they've never needed before, what would be your first step?"

These questions don't just assess skills; they reveal how candidates think, adapt, and align with your team's culture. By using scenarios like the Bisleri example, you can identify the candidates who will excel in the unpredictable, high-pressure world of BDR work.

Crafting Effective Job Descriptions

Writing a job description isn't just about listing duties; it's your first chance to sell the role and the company to potential candidates. A compelling job description should make the role feel exciting, impactful, and worth pursuing. It's not about overselling or making grandiose promises—it's about painting a clear picture of the opportunity while igniting curiosity and ambition.

Chapter 1: Setting Up a BDR Team

A BDR job description is more than a laundry list of tasks. It's your pitch to individuals who are ready to grow, face challenges, and contribute meaningfully. It should inspire candidates to imagine the impact they can make while showing them a path for their own professional development.

What Makes a Great Job Description?
- **Clarity Over Fluff**
  Avoid buzzwords that add no substance (no one wants to join a team of "superstars"). Instead, focus on providing clarity about the role and its importance to the company.
  - Example: Instead of "We're looking for a people person," say: "You'll engage with prospects to understand their challenges and communicate how our solutions address their needs."
- **Show the Big Picture**
  Help candidates see how the role fits into the company's larger goals. A BDR isn't just cold-calling; they're building the foundation of the company's future growth.
  - Example: "As a BDR, you'll play a critical role in driving pipeline generation and directly influencing our success in new markets."
- **Highlight Growth Opportunities**
  Make it clear that this role isn't a dead end. Mention opportunities to transition into roles like Account Executive, Customer Success Manager, or Revenue Operations. Candidates with ambition will gravitate to roles where they can see a future.
- **Make It Human**
  Your job description should sound like it was written by a person, not a machine. Show some personality, reflect your company culture, and avoid sounding overly corporate.
  - Example: "Join a team that celebrates creativity and encourages experimentation to find new ways of solving problems."

Example Job Description
"We're searching for a driven Business Development Representative to help shape the future of our sales pipeline. You'll identify, qualify, and nurture new opportunities while developing the skills to become a future leader. If you thrive on connecting with people, solving problems, and sparking meaningful conversations, this role is for you."

"As a BDR, you'll work closely with our sales and marketing teams to bring in fresh opportunities and build a strong foundation for our company's growth. We'll provide you with the tools, mentorship, and training to excel in this role and prepare for your next step, whether it's becoming an Account Executive, joining our RevOps team, or pursuing other leadership roles."

Chapter 1: Setting Up a BDR Team

Essential Components of a Job Description
- **The Opening Hook**
  Start with a statement that grabs attention and immediately answers: Why should I care about this role?
  - Example: "Do you love connecting with people, uncovering their needs, and creating solutions that make a difference? Join us as a Business Development Representative and be the first face of our brand to potential customers."
- **Responsibilities That Matter**
  Avoid generic tasks like "Make calls" or "Generate leads." Focus instead on responsibilities that highlight the role's impact:
  - Research and identify key decision-makers in target industries.
  - Craft personalized outreach to engage potential clients and spark interest.
  - Partner with sales and marketing teams to refine messaging and strategies.
- **What They'll Gain**
  Clearly outline what the candidate will achieve and learn in the role:
  - Develop critical skills in prospecting, relationship-building, and sales strategy.
  - Gain exposure to tools like CRM systems and sales engagement platforms.
  - Work alongside a team that values growth, creativity, and collaboration.
- **Who You're Looking For**
  Describe the ideal candidate in terms of traits and attitudes, not just skills:
  - Someone curious, adaptable, and eager to learn.
  - A self-starter who thrives in fast-paced environments.
  - An excellent communicator who can build trust and connect with prospects.

Avoiding Common Pitfalls

Too Many Requirements
Don't scare off candidates by listing unrealistic qualifications like "5+ years of experience in sales." This can deter talented individuals who have the drive but lack traditional experience.

Instead, focus on core traits like curiosity, resilience, and problem-solving skills. These are the qualities that define success in the BDR role. A great BDR can come from any background—what matters is their eagerness to learn, adapt, and succeed.

Vague or Generic Language
If your job description looks like it could fit any company, you've missed the mark. Tailor it to reflect your company's unique culture, values, and mission. Candidates want to know who you are and why they should join you.

Recruitment Strategies

Chapter 1: Setting Up a BDR Team

Example:
"Join a team that celebrates creativity and encourages experimentation to find new ways of solving problems."

This gives candidates a sense of your culture and shows them that their contributions will be valued.

Overpromising
Be honest about what the role involves. If the day-to-day includes rejection, repetition, and overcoming challenges, say so—but frame it in a way that highlights the growth and rewards that come with perseverance.

Example:
"Your days will involve reaching out to prospects, handling objections, and navigating rejection. But every 'no' gets you closer to a 'yes,' and the skills you'll develop along the way will serve you throughout your career."

Why Job Descriptions Matter

Your job description isn't just a formality; it's the start of your relationship with a future team member. A great one sets the tone for their experience with your company and ensures you attract the right people—those who are excited, prepared, and ready to contribute.

Crafting job descriptions with intention ensures you're not just filling seats but building a team that drives success. The best candidates aren't just looking for a job—they're looking for an opportunity to grow, make an impact, and be part of something meaningful.

Your job description is the first step in showing them that your company is the place where that happens.

Chapter 1: Setting Up a BDR Team

The 30, 60, 90-Day Onboarding Plan

Overview
Onboarding isn't just about teaching new hires how to use tools or write a cold email. It's about laying the groundwork for long-term success, turning rookies into confident and productive team members. Think of it like preparing for a marathon: you don't start with a sprint—you build endurance, refine your technique, and ensure your team is ready for the challenges ahead.

Here's a breakdown of how to structure onboarding effectively, with real-world examples to make the process relatable and actionable.

The First 30 Days: Laying the Foundation
Focus: Familiarize new hires with tools, processes, and your team's culture. Build their confidence and establish early expectations.

- **Tools and Systems:**
  Gradually introduce the tech stack, starting with essentials like the CRM and sales engagement platforms.
  Example: *New hires begin with dummy leads in a simulated CRM environment, practicing data input, task scheduling, and follow-ups. This hands-on training, combined with shadowing top performers, allows them to learn the nuances of tools like LinkedIn Sales Navigator in a low-pressure setting. The result? A smoother transition to live operations with fewer errors.*

- **Role-Playing and Scenario Practice:**
  Use role-playing to prepare new hires for real-world scenarios.
  Example Scenario:
  A prospect says, "I'm not interested. Stop calling me."
  Encourage new hires to try responses such as:
    - *"I understand. Before I let you go, can I ask what's missing for you in our solution?"*
    - *"I hear you. Just curious, has something changed since our last conversation?"*

  Real-time feedback during these exercises helps pinpoint areas for improvement.

- **The Buddy Program:**
  Pair new hires with experienced team members for a safe learning environment.
  Example: A SaaS company's buddy program allowed new hires to shadow live calls during their first week. Post-call debriefs clarified what worked, what didn't, and why. One new hire remarked, "*It was like having a cheat sheet for real-world situations,*" leading to faster ramp-up times and stronger first-call performance.

Chapter 1: Setting Up a BDR Team

Day 31 to 60: Skill Development
Focus: Refine skills through exposure, practice, and feedback.

- **Team Call-Listening Sessions:**
  Analyze real calls to identify best practices and common pitfalls.
  Example: A tech startup's team reviewed contrasting call recordings—one was a perfect pitch, and the other was a misstep where the BDR confused the prospect's company name. The exercise highlighted the importance of preparation and resulted in a 15% improvement in first-call effectiveness.

- **Shadowing Top Performers:**
  Letting new hires observe seasoned BDRs helps them grasp nuances like handling objections or adapting to tone shifts.
  Example: A top performer used humor to break the ice with a hesitant prospect. A new hire replicated the approach, booking their first meeting with a tough lead.

- **Collaborative Problem-Solving:**
  Group exercises foster camaraderie and critical thinking.
  Example Challenge:
  "You've been handed a list of 50 dormant leads. How would you re-engage them?"
  Teams brainstormed ideas like a "We Missed You" campaign or personalized LinkedIn messages referencing company updates. One group proposed sending coffee gift cards with the tagline, *"Let's chat over coffee!"* The creative exercise inspired actionable ideas adopted across the team.

Day 61 to 90: Independent Operation
Focus: Autonomy and ownership.

New hires should feel confident running their outreach campaigns while still benefiting from structured coaching and support. This stage emphasizes accountability and measurable contributions to the pipeline, while also celebrating milestones to keep morale high.

- **Ownership of Outreach**
  Empower new hires to take full ownership of their campaigns, from strategy to execution, while ensuring coaching and feedback remain accessible.
  Example:
  A BDR at a SaaS company was tasked with reviving a dormant lead. Through research, they discovered the prospect's company had recently launched a new product line. Using this insight, the BDR crafted a personalized email tying the product launch to their solution. The email secured a meeting, marking their first deal-ready opportunity.

Chapter 1: Setting Up a BDR Team

This approach demonstrates how autonomy, combined with ongoing feedback, enables new hires to apply their training effectively and confidently.

- **Weekly Coaching Sessions**
  Regular one-on-one check-ins remain crucial in this phase. Coaching provides a safety net, allowing new hires to discuss challenges and refine their approach.
  Example:
  During a weekly coaching session, a manager noticed that a BDR was struggling with time management. Together, they developed a daily schedule prioritizing high-value tasks, such as reaching out to top-tier leads in the morning. Within two weeks, the BDR doubled their call volume while maintaining outreach quality.

  These coaching sessions not only reinforce skills but also build trust and accountability between managers and team members.

- **Gamify Milestones**
  Gamification can boost engagement and morale during this phase, turning daily tasks into opportunities for celebration and camaraderie.
  Example:
  At one company, new hires participated in a "First 50 Calls" challenge. The first to hit the milestone received a small prize, such as a gift card, while everyone who completed it earned team-wide recognition. This simple game fostered friendly competition, energized the team, and gave new hires a sense of accomplishment early on.

Wrapping Up the Onboarding Plan
By the end of Day 90, new BDRs should:
- Feel confident managing their own campaigns.
- Demonstrate measurable contributions to the pipeline (e.g., meetings booked, leads qualified).
- Be fully integrated into team workflows and culture.

Onboarding doesn't stop at Day 90—it transitions into ongoing development. Regular coaching, collaborative problem-solving, and recognition of achievements ensure that BDRs continue to grow and deliver value well beyond their first three months.

Chapter 1: Setting Up a BDR Team

Essential Tools and Resources

Your BDR team's success doesn't rely solely on their skills—it's also about equipping them with the right tools. In today's competitive landscape, a robust tech stack isn't just a nice-to-have; it's essential. From managing workflows to enhancing outreach, these tools streamline processes and give your team the edge they need to excel.

The Must-Have Tools for BDR Success

- **Customer Relationship Management (CRM):**
  A CRM is the backbone of any sales team. Tools like HubSpot or Salesforce store every interaction, log follow-ups, and keep the pipeline organized.
  - Why It Matters: A well-utilized CRM ensures no prospect is ever forgotten, allowing your team to focus on meaningful outreach rather than administrative tasks.

- **Sales Engagement Platforms:**
  Platforms like Outreach.io or Salesloft help automate multi-channel outreach and track engagement, making follow-ups seamless.
  - Why It Matters: These platforms ensure your team stays consistent while still personalizing their communication.

- **Video Prospecting Tools:**
  Personalization is key, and nothing grabs attention quite like video. Tools like Vidyard and Loom allow BDRs to create short, customized videos, adding a human touch to their outreach.
  - Example: A BDR at a SaaS company used Vidyard to send a personalized video to a prospect, highlighting how their product could address a specific pain point. The result? A meeting booked within 24 hours.

- **Intent Data Tools:**
  Tools like 6sense, Bombora, or Factors provide insights into buying intent by tracking online behavior and engagement patterns.
  - Why It Matters: Knowing when a prospect is actively searching for solutions gives your team an edge, allowing them to prioritize high-potential leads.

- **Prospecting Tools:**
  Platforms like LinkedIn Sales Navigator, Apollo.io, and ZoomInfo are invaluable for finding decision-makers, mapping company hierarchies, and gathering key insights.
  - Why It Matters: These tools simplify crafting highly personalized outreach strategies.

- **Call Analytics and Coaching Software:**
  Tools like Gong.io and Chorus.ai analyze calls to identify trends, highlight opportunities, and provide coaching insights.

Chapter 1: Setting Up a BDR Team

- ○ Why It Matters: They're invaluable for improving team performance and refining scripts.

- **Pipeline Visibility and Forecasting Tools:**
  Tools like Clari or InsightSquared provide visibility into pipeline health, allowing managers and BDRs to track progress and identify gaps.
  - ○ Why It Matters: These insights enable more strategic decision-making and resource allocation.
- **Email Warm-Up and Deliverability Tools:**
  Tools like Mailshake and Lemlist ensure your team's emails avoid spam folders. They help optimize deliverability and track engagement metrics, such as opens and clicks.

Subconscious Tool Adoption: A Long-Term Success Strategy
Introducing tools to your BDR team should feel like adding pieces to a puzzle, not overwhelming them all at once. The gradual adoption of tools creates seamless integration into daily workflows. By layering tools into the team's routine, you ensure they view these tools as indispensable parts of their process.

How to Drive Adoption:
- **Integrate Tools into Coaching and Feedback:**
  Refer to insights derived from tools during coaching sessions. For example, use call analytics data to pinpoint improvement areas or celebrate specific wins tied to engagement metrics.
- **Incorporate Tools into Team Rituals:**
  - ○ Use CRM insights during stand-ups to highlight prospect progress.
  - ○ Share engagement platform data during strategy sessions to refine campaigns.
- **Gamify Tool Usage:**
  Create small challenges, such as "Log all calls in the CRM for a week without missing follow-ups," and reward consistency.
- **Provide Context for Each Tool:**
  Show how each tool solves a specific challenge. For instance:
  - ○ Use video prospecting to break through email fatigue.
  - ○ Leverage intent data to time outreach perfectly.
- **Normalize Peer Interaction Around Tools:**
  Encourage BDRs to share success stories tied to tool usage.
  - ○ Example: "Using LinkedIn Sales Navigator, I identified a prospect's pain point and secured a meeting."

By equipping your team with the right tools and introducing them thoughtfully, you ensure not just adoption but mastery. Tools become less about "what to use" and more about "how we succeed," seamlessly blending into workflows to drive consistent results.

Chapter 1: Setting Up a BDR Team

Creating an Ecosystem of Necessity

Subconscious tool adoption happens when BDRs can't imagine their workflows without the tools. The key is to make tools indispensable, seamlessly integrating them into everyday processes. To achieve this, leaders must take intentional steps that position tools as essential allies, not optional extras.

Lead by Example
Use the tools yourself in team reviews, one-on-ones, and reporting. Demonstrate their value by relying on them to make decisions, share insights, and provide feedback. When BDRs see you using tools to drive performance, they'll naturally follow suit.

Position Tools as Time-Savers, Not Time-Wasters
Emphasize how tools streamline tedious tasks and free up time for meaningful work. BDRs are more likely to embrace tools when they view them as allies that simplify their day.
Example:
- A prospecting platform eliminates hours of manual research by surfacing decision-makers and their contact details in minutes.

Praise Tool-Driven Wins
Publicly celebrate achievements that result from effective tool use. Whether it's a meeting booked through insights from a prospecting platform or a key takeaway from a call analytics tool, connect the win to the tool that enabled it.

Introduce Tools in Context
Don't just explain what a tool does—demonstrate how it solves specific challenges.
Examples:
- A video prospecting tool can break through email fatigue, capturing attention with a personalized touch.
- A CRM workflow simplifies follow-ups, ensuring prospects are nurtured effectively.

When tools are positioned as solutions to real problems, they become relevant and immediately valuable.

Subtle Reinforcement Through Habit-Building
Habits form when behaviors are repeated consistently within a framework of reinforcement. These strategies help build tool usage into your team's daily routine:
- **Start Small:**
  Introduce one critical feature of a tool at a time. For example, begin with logging calls in the CRM before exploring advanced reporting features. Incremental mastery builds confidence and familiarity.

Chapter 1: Setting Up a BDR Team

- **Embed Tools into Processes:**
  Align tools with mandatory workflows. For instance, require that all follow-ups be logged in the CRM before a deal moves to the next stage. When the tool becomes synonymous with completing a task, its usage becomes automatic.
- **Provide Consistent Feedback Loops:**
  Regularly review how tools are being used and share insights.
  Example: "Our email engagement tool shows that response rates improve by 20% when subject lines are under 40 characters." Feedback like this reinforces the utility of the tool and encourages continued use.

Why Subconscious Adoption Matters
When tools are subconsciously embedded in workflows, they cease to feel like external systems and become integral to how the team operates. This doesn't just increase adoption rates—it transforms tools into drivers of efficiency, productivity, and growth.

Your BDRs won't just use the tools because they have to; they'll use them because they can't imagine doing their job without them.

With the right tools in place and a strategy for gradual, subconscious adoption, your team is primed for success.

Chapter 1: Setting Up a BDR Team

Setting Early Expectations

Establishing clear expectations isn't just about setting quotas or KPIs; it's about creating a shared understanding of what success looks like from the start. Without clarity, your BDRs might feel like they're wandering in the dark, unsure of what's expected or how to measure their progress.
Setting the tone early gives your team a roadmap to follow and the confidence to excel.

Why Expectations Matter
When BDRs know exactly what's expected of them—both in terms of metrics and behavior—they're more likely to stay motivated and focused. Expectations act as guardrails, helping your team avoid aimless activity while fostering accountability.
Ambiguity, on the other hand, breeds inconsistency and frustration. Clear expectations align individual efforts with team objectives, ensuring that everyone moves in the same direction.

Components of Early Expectations
- **Quantitative Goals**
  Metrics like calls made, emails sent, and meetings booked are the backbone of a BDR's day-to-day responsibilities. These goals should be realistic yet challenging, providing a clear target to aim for.
  Example: "Aim for 40 calls, 10 personalized emails, and 2 booked meetings per day."
- Example: "For inbound leads, follow up within 24 hours and log all interactions in the CRM."
- **Qualitative Expectations**
  It's not just about hitting numbers—it's about how they approach their work. Set expectations for professionalism, communication, and the quality of their outreach.
  A poorly written email may count toward a goal, but it won't deliver results. Encourage attention to detail and relevance in all communications.
- **Behavioral Norms**
  Reinforce the importance of curiosity, resilience, and adaptability. Make it clear that learning from mistakes is valued over perfection and encourage BDRs to seek feedback actively.
  Example: "If a prospect rejects your outreach, take note of their objections and adjust your approach for the next attempt."

Setting the Foundation from Day One

Daily Routines and KPIs
Define what a productive day looks like by breaking down tasks into manageable chunks tied to specific outcomes.

Chapter 1: Setting Up a BDR Team

- Example: "Every day, aim for 10 calls to top-tier prospects, 30 additional outreach attempts, and follow up on 3 warm leads."
- Example: "Ensure all lead interactions are logged in the CRM to maintain pipeline accuracy."

Tools Integration into Expectations
Subtly tie expectations to tool usage:
- Example: "Track email performance using the engagement platform to refine messaging."
- Example: "Log all call outcomes in the CRM immediately after each conversation."

Mindset Over Metrics
Highlight the importance of a growth mindset over raw numbers.
- Example: "If you make 40 calls and 10 connect, focus on what you learned from those calls rather than the rejections."
- Example: "Experiment with outreach techniques and share your findings with the team."

Reinforcing Expectations Through Check-Ins

Daily Stand-Ups
Use quick 10-minute morning huddles to:
- Set the tone for the day.
- Share insights or success stories from the previous day.
- Encourage BDRs to state their goals for the day.
- Revisit those goals the next morning to create accountability.

Weekly One-on-Ones
Dive deeper during individual check-ins to:
- Review performance against KPIs.
- Discuss challenges and brainstorm solutions.
- Celebrate wins—big or small—to build confidence and reinforce progress.

Team Meetings
Weekly team sessions align goals and encourage collaboration:
- Highlight how individual and team expectations tie into broader objectives.
- Share examples of exceptional outreach or innovative strategies.

Handling Pushback and Resistance
Not every BDR will embrace expectations immediately. Resistance often stems from a lack of understanding or confidence. Address this by:
- **Explaining the Why:** Show how their goals contribute to team success and personal growth.

Chapter 1: Setting Up a BDR Team

- Offering Support: Reinforce that you're there to help, not just evaluate. Provide coaching, resources, and encouragement.
- Adapting When Necessary: If expectations aren't realistic, adjust them based on data and feedback. Unrealistic goals kill morale; achievable ones inspire performance.

Aligning Expectations with Team Culture

Expectations aren't just about numbers; they're about the culture you want to build. Reinforce values like:
- Mistakes as opportunities to learn, not failures.
- Collaboration and knowledge-sharing as important as individual success.
- Curiosity and experimentation—even if they don't always lead to immediate wins.

The Feedback Loop

Early expectations shouldn't be static; they should evolve based on what works and what doesn't. Create a feedback loop to refine expectations:
- Regularly analyze performance data to identify trends.
- Gather input from your team during check-ins and team meetings.
- Adjust goals and processes to keep them challenging yet attainable.

The Long-Term Impact of Clear Expectations
Setting early expectations is about more than getting your team started on the right foot—it's about shaping a mindset and culture that pays dividends long after the initial training period. Expectations are the invisible scaffolding that supports your team's growth, performance, and morale.

When done right, they don't just set the tone for the first 90 days—they create a foundation for sustained success.

Long-Term Benefits of Clear Expectations:
- Building a Culture of Accountability
- Fostering a Growth Mindset
- Providing Consistency in a Changing Environment
- Strengthening Team Cohesion
- Elevating Performance Over Time
- Enhancing Manager-Rep Relationships
- Driving Better Results

By setting expectations early and reinforcing them consistently, you're not just guiding your team through their first 90 days—you're laying the groundwork for a career of continuous improvement and success.

Chapter 2: Setting Targets and KPIs

Let's be honest: targets and KPIs are the lifeblood of any sales team. Without them, your BDRs might as well be throwing spaghetti at the wall to see what sticks. Targets provide the "what," and KPIs provide the "how"—together, they form the GPS system for your team. And just like a GPS, they'll reroute your team when they take a wrong turn (like sending their 10th follow-up email to a prospect who said, "Take me off your list!" three emails ago).

But targets and KPIs aren't just about cracking the whip or being a spreadsheet enthusiast. They're about science, psychology, and motivation. When set and communicated correctly, they align your team's efforts with broader business goals, create a sense of purpose, and, yes, even improve morale (because nothing feels better than smashing a target).

The Science Behind Why Targets and KPIs Work

Goal-Setting Theory
Psychologists Edwin Locke and Gary Latham established that setting specific, challenging goals leads to higher performance than vague, easy-to-reach ones. Why? Because the brain loves clarity and rewards effort with a dopamine hit when goals are achieved.

"Book 10 meetings this week" beats the vague "go get some leads." A BDR with clear targets knows exactly what success looks like. They don't waste energy wondering, "Am I doing enough?" Their focus shifts from figuring out what to do to actually doing it.

Behavioral Economics
People are naturally loss-averse, meaning they'll work harder to avoid falling short of a target than to exceed one by a wide margin. Targets trigger this response by creating a defined finish line. Missing that line feels like a loss, even if the effort was strong.

If a BDR is given a clear target of 12 meetings a month, they'll push harder to hit 12 than if you vaguely encourage them to *"book as many as you can."* The fear of underperforming activates their internal drive.

The Zeigarnik Effect
Named after psychologist Bluma Zeigarnik, this principle states that humans remember incomplete tasks better than completed ones. Clear targets leverage this effect by keeping unachieved goals top of mind, nudging your team to prioritize unfinished work.

A BDR who has booked 9 meetings by the 25th of the month will feel the internal pull to push for that 10th meeting before month-end, even if it means staying a little late or trying a creative outreach method.

Chapter 2: Setting Targets and KPIs

Clarity: The Secret Ingredient
Targets and KPIs remove ambiguity, which is the silent killer of productivity. A BDR without clear goals is like someone walking into a gym without a plan—they might lift a few weights, jog a little, and leave feeling like they've accomplished something, but there's no measurable progress.

Instead of: *"Focus on outreach this week."*
Say: *"Send 50 personalized emails and make 30 calls to enterprise accounts this week."*

Why does this work? Because specific goals activate the brain's planning and reward systems. The clarity eliminates guesswork, leaving BDRs to focus on execution rather than interpretation.

Humor Meets Science: Why KPIs Save Leaders' Sanity
Picture this: it's the end of the quarter, and your CEO asks why the pipeline looks thinner than your morning coffee. Without KPIs, you'd shrug and mumble something about "low activity." With KPIs, you pull up a dashboard, point to where the calls dropped off, and identify where the pipeline bottlenecked. Science and sarcasm combine to save the day.

KPIs allow you to spot patterns, like:
- *"Why are we making 100 calls a day but only booking 2 meetings? Are we calling wrong numbers or accidentally insulting prospects' pets?"*
- *"Why is the email open rate 5% lower this month? Did we suddenly forget how to write subject lines?"*

The data doesn't lie—it's your cheat sheet to identifying problems, coaching effectively, and tweaking strategy.

The Emotional Boost of Hitting Targets
Let's talk dopamine, the brain's feel-good chemical. Achieving a target triggers a dopamine release, creating a sense of accomplishment. This isn't just motivational fluff; it's biology. A well-hit target feels as satisfying as the first sip of coffee on a Monday morning (or the end of a brutal cold call where the prospect actually says, *"Sure, let's talk!"*).
- For BDRs: Hitting targets makes their work feel meaningful and reinforces their confidence.
- For Leaders: A team consistently hitting KPIs is the dream. It means the process is working, and you're not losing sleep over pipeline gaps.

The Long-Term Impact: Targets That Teach
The best targets aren't just about numbers—they teach discipline, consistency, and problem-solving. A BDR chasing 12 meetings a month learns to manage their time, analyze what works, and push themselves creatively. Those lessons don't just

The Science Behind Why Targets and KPIs Work

Chapter 2: Setting Targets and KPIs

boost current performance; they build skills that prepare them for future roles, whether in AE, RevOps, or leadership.

In Summary: Why Targets and KPIs Are Non-Negotiable

Targets and KPIs are often misunderstood as tools for micromanagement. In reality, they're the antithesis of micromanagement—they liberate your team by providing purpose, direction, and autonomy. Instead of wandering aimlessly, unsure of what to prioritize, your BDRs can approach each day with clarity and focus, knowing exactly how their efforts align with broader goals.

Managing Purpose, Not Just Metrics
A target is more than just a number; it's a mission. When a BDR is tasked with booking 12 meetings in a month, that target becomes their guiding star. It's not about checking boxes—it's about understanding why those 12 meetings matter. They're not just dialing phones or sending emails; they're directly contributing to the company's pipeline and future revenue.

KPIs, on the other hand, act like the mile markers on a marathon route. They tell your team whether they're on pace or falling behind, offering the reassurance of progress or the motivation to pick up speed. By connecting activity to outcomes, KPIs transform abstract goals into actionable steps.

The Ripple Effect on the Team
When productivity meets purpose, it doesn't just benefit individual BDRs—it transforms the entire team dynamic. A group of aligned, motivated BDRs generates positive energy, which is contagious. Collaboration flourishes, wins are celebrated, and challenges are tackled with a shared determination. Targets and KPIs create a culture where success isn't just an expectation—it's a habit.
The Bigger Picture

At their core, targets and KPIs are about creating meaning in the day-to-day grind. They remind your BDRs that their work matters, their efforts drive results, and their success is part of a larger story. When you manage with purpose rather than pressure, you don't just hit numbers—you build a team that thrives.

By embedding targets and KPIs into your BDR operation, you're not just setting goals; you're setting the stage for sustained performance, growth, and success.

Chapter 2: Setting Targets and KPIs

Activity vs. Outcome Metrics

Let's clear something up: not all metrics are created equal. Some are the fuel for your team's engine, while others are the end destination. Understanding the difference between activity metrics and outcome metrics—and knowing how to balance them—is the secret to running a BDR team that doesn't just move, but moves with purpose.

Activity Metrics
Activity metrics track what your team does. They're the calls, emails, LinkedIn connections, and follow-ups that fill a BDR's day. These are the things they can control.

Outcome Metrics
Outcome metrics, on the other hand, measure what your team achieves—meetings booked, opportunities created, and pipeline generated. These are the results of their effort, influenced by both their actions and external factors.

The Key to Success
Treat activity metrics like the ingredients for a great dish and outcome metrics as the finished meal. Without the right balance, you'll either end up overworking your team with little to show for it or underestimating the effort needed to hit those pipeline goals.

The Science of Activity Metrics
Humans love quick wins—it's how our brains are wired. Every time a BDR ticks off a completed task, the brain releases dopamine, the feel-good chemical. This makes activity metrics powerful motivators, especially for early-career reps still building their confidence.

But activity metrics alone can become busywork. If your team is making 100 calls a day but only converting 2% of them into meetings, something is broken. You've got a lot of noise but not much music. This is why activity metrics should always be viewed as a means to an end, not the end itself.

The Real Talk on Outcome Metrics
Outcome metrics are where the magic (or frustration) happens. They measure the things that actually move the needle for your company—meetings booked, opportunities created, pipeline generated.

Here's the catch: Outcomes are influenced by factors beyond a BDR's control, like market conditions, the quality of the leads they're working with, or even the mood of a prospect on a given day.

Chapter 2: Setting Targets and KPIs

Focusing only on outcome metrics can feel unfair to your team. A BDR could be doing everything right—crafting personalized emails, delivering pitch-perfect calls—but still fall short if they're handed a bad lead list. That's why outcome metrics should be the North Star, not the hammer you swing every time numbers dip.

Balancing Activity and Outcome Metrics
Activity metrics are the "how," and outcome metrics are the "why." A high-performing BDR team doesn't just grind out activities; they execute them with precision and purpose, driving toward meaningful outcomes.

For Example:
- Activity Metric: Make 50 calls a day.
- Outcome Metric: Book 5 qualified meetings a week.

If the team consistently hits activity metrics but falls short on outcomes, it's a signal that something needs to be recalibrated—whether it's the messaging, the target accounts, or the qualification process.

Common Pitfalls to Avoid
- **Overemphasizing Activity**
  Pushing for sky-high call or email numbers without focusing on quality leads to burnout and inefficiency. If a BDR is hitting 100 calls a day but only getting one conversation, it's time to rethink the approach.
- **Overemphasizing Outcomes**
  Setting aggressive booking targets without considering activity levels creates a black hole of expectations. Your team won't know whether they're underperforming or simply under-supported.
- **Neglecting Feedback Loops**
  Metrics should inform adjustments, not just sit in a dashboard. If you're not using activity data to improve outcomes, you're missing the point.

Tying It All Together
Activity metrics keep your team accountable for what they can control. Outcome metrics keep them focused on what matters most. The sweet spot lies in using activity metrics as early indicators of success and outcome metrics as the validation of your strategy.

Together, these metrics don't just tell you what's happening—they tell you why it's happening. And when your team understands both, they don't just grind—they grow.

Activity vs. Outcome Metrics Across Scenarios
Metrics aren't one-size-fits-all. The balance between activity and outcome metrics—and the type of metrics you emphasize—changes based on the team's focus, the market you're targeting, and the product you're selling.

Chapter 2: Setting Targets and KPIs

- **Onboarding new reps?** Activity metrics dominate.
- **Running an inbound team?** Outcome metrics take center stage.
- **Outbound?** You need a nuanced mix of both.

Onboarding: Building Confidence Through Activities
For new hires, especially during their onboarding phase, the emphasis should be on activity metrics. Reps need to build habits, develop muscle memory, and get comfortable with the tools and processes before being held accountable for outcomes.

Activity Metrics for Onboarding
- Daily Calls: 20 calls to practice tone, scripts, and objection handling.
- Email Drafts Reviewed: Submit 5 personalized email drafts per week for feedback.
- CRM Hygiene: Log 100% of daily activities to ensure they master the system.
- Role-Plays Completed: Participate in 3 mock calls or email reviews weekly.

Outcome Metrics for Onboarding (Light Touch)
- First Meeting Booked: Celebrate their first booked meeting, even if it takes extra support.
- Call Connection Rate: Aim for a modest 5-10% connection rate in the first month as they refine their approach.

Why It's Different in Onboarding
Here, the focus is on mastery and repetition, not immediate pipeline contribution. You're teaching them to crawl before they sprint.

Inbound Team: Converting Interest into Action
Inbound teams operate in a warmer environment where prospects have already shown some level of interest. This makes outcome metrics more critical, as the goal is to capitalize on leads efficiently. However, activity metrics still matter for speed and consistency.

Activity Metrics for Inbound Teams
- Response Time: Follow up on inbound leads within 1 hour of receipt.
- Daily Outreach: Contact 15 inbound leads per day via phone, email, or LinkedIn.
- Follow-Up Cadence: Ensure every inbound lead receives at least 3 touchpoints within a week.

Outcome Metrics for Inbound Teams
- Qualification Rate: Qualify 50% of inbound leads into meetings.
- Meeting Conversion Rate: Convert 70% of qualified leads into meetings with AEs.
- Pipeline Contribution: Generate $500K in pipeline per quarter from inbound leads.

Chapter 2: Setting Targets and KPIs

Why It's Different for Inbound Teams
The leads are already warmer, so there's less reliance on heavy activity volumes. The focus shifts to speed, quality, and maximizing conversion rates.

Outbound Team: Creating Demand from Scratch
Outbound teams face a tougher landscape—they're reaching out cold, building relationships, and sparking interest where none existed. This requires a balanced mix of activity and outcome metrics, leaning slightly heavier on activities to ensure consistent effort.

Activity Metrics for Outbound Teams
- **Daily Calls:** 50-70 calls to cold leads, depending on market size and target personas.
- **Email Sequences Sent:** 25 personalized emails per day.
- **Account Research Time:** Spend 1-2 hours daily researching target accounts to craft personalized outreach.
- **LinkedIn Connections:** Add 10 new connections per day to build social selling pipelines.

Outcome Metrics for Outbound Teams
- **Meetings Booked:** Book 8-10 meetings per month with target accounts.
- **Opportunity Conversion Rate:** Convert 20% of meetings into qualified opportunities.
- **Account Penetration Rate:** Reach decision-makers in 30% of target accounts.
- **Pipeline Value:** Generate $250K in pipeline per quarter.

Why It's Different for Outbound Teams
In cold outreach, effort drives results. Activity consistency builds momentum, while outcome metrics ensure that activities are effective.

Customization by Market and Product
The type of market (enterprise, SMB, or mid-market) and the product you're selling (low ACV, high ACV, niche, or broad appeal) significantly influence your metric balance.

For Enterprise Markets
Enterprise deals often have longer sales cycles and involve multiple stakeholders, so quality over quantity is key.
- **Activity Metric:** Focus on multi-threading—engage 3-5 stakeholders per account.
- **Outcome Metric:** Book 3 high-quality meetings per month, with a focus on strategic accounts.

For SMB Markets
SMBs have faster cycles but higher volumes, so activity levels are crucial.

Activity vs. Outcome Metrics

Chapter 2: Setting Targets and KPIs

- Activity Metric: 70 calls per day with quick follow-ups.
- Outcome Metric: Book 12-15 meetings per month, prioritizing speed over deep personalization.

For High-ACV Products
Selling high-ticket solutions requires a consultative approach.
- Activity Metric: Spend 2 hours daily researching target accounts and building hyper-personalized outreach.
- Outcome Metric: Book 6 meetings per month with a pipeline value exceeding $100K.

For Low-ACV Products
Lower-value deals require scale.
- Activity Metric: 100 calls or 50 emails daily to maximize volume.
- Outcome Metric: Book 20 meetings per month with a smaller pipeline target per deal.

Key Takeaway
Activity and outcome metrics must reflect the reality of your team's role, market, and product. Outbound teams grind harder upfront, while inbound teams refine conversion efficiency. Enterprise markets demand patience, while SMBs reward speed. The art of leadership lies in tailoring these metrics to match the context, keeping your team productive and focused without losing sight of the bigger picture.

Flexibility is key as your company grows. Early-stage companies might emphasize meeting targets to drive initial momentum, but as the organization scales, the focus should shift toward qualified opportunities, pipeline value, and even small stakes in closed revenue.

This progression aligns metrics with evolving business needs, keeping BDRs invested in outcomes that genuinely move the needle, while rewarding creativity and ownership at every stage.

This matrix offers a clear visualization of performance zones, highlighting how "Busy But Lost" efforts and the "Burnout Zone" can sap productivity and morale. The goal is to steer your team toward the "Strategic Performer" quadrant, where high activity is aligned with high outcomes.

Chapter 2: Setting Targets and KPIs

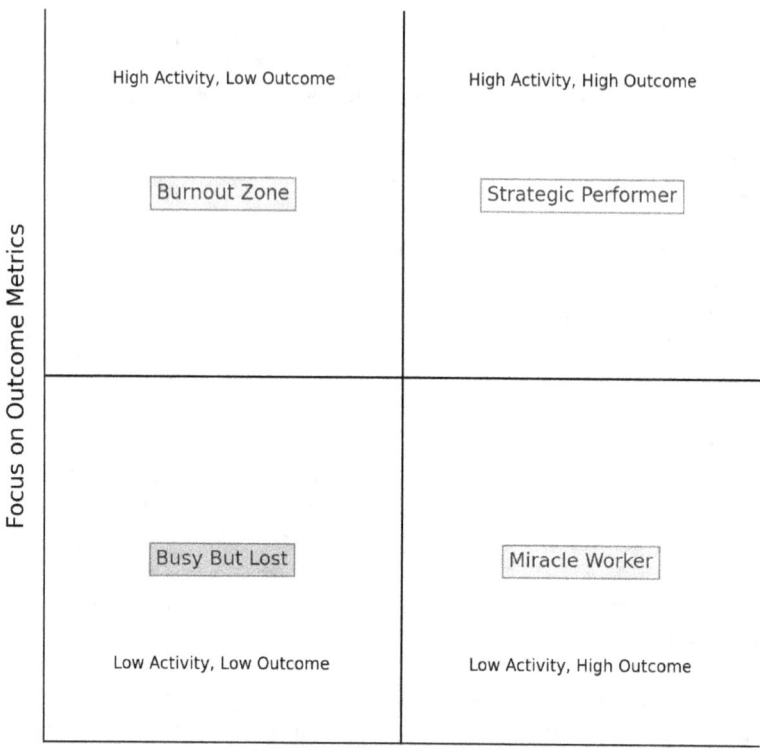

Avoid the trap of relying on "Miracle Worker" luck, as it often leads to inconsistent results. Instead, focus on fostering sustainable strategies that drive predictable, long-term success.

Chapter 2: Setting Targets and KPIs

The Art and Science of Quotas

Quotas are like a fitness tracker for your BDR team: when designed thoughtfully, they provide structure, drive progress, and maybe even make you feel a little guilty if you don't hit them. The best quotas do more than just measure performance—they challenge, motivate, and (occasionally) make you sweat.

Balancing the art and science of quota-setting is key. Too much science, and your team might feel like lab rats. Too much art, and they'll wonder if hitting their numbers depends on aligning with Mercury in retrograde. The right mix drives results while keeping your team energized and engaged.

The Science: Data-Driven Clarity

Let's start with the "don't-blame-me-this-is-math" side of quotas. Hard data removes ambiguity and gives your team clear, actionable goals. By analyzing historical performance and market realities, you ensure quotas are grounded in reality—not in your wildest dreams.

- **Historical Trends:** Look at past performance for a reality check. If the team averaged 8 meetings/month last quarter, don't set the next goal at 20 (unless you enjoy mass resignations). Aiming for 10-12 is ambitious but fair.
- **Conversion Rates:** Reverse-engineer your quotas based on funnel data:
    - How many calls lead to conversations?
    - How many conversations lead to meetings?
    - How many meetings lead to deals?
    - Pro tip: if you're not tracking these, your quotas are probably fueled by optimism alone.
- **Market Realities:** Not all markets are created equal.
    - For SMBs, prioritize volume and activity metrics (e.g., calls made).
    - For enterprise accounts, focus on high-quality meetings with decision-makers.
    - Example: For enterprise, setting 6 meetings/month beats 12 random calls that result in crickets.
- **Growth Stage:** Early-stage companies thrive on activity (think: lots of calls and emails). Mature companies should tie quotas more closely to pipeline and revenue.

The Art: Psychology and Motivation

Numbers are necessary, but they won't exactly get your team out of bed in the morning. The art of quota-setting is about connecting the dots between the grind and the glory.

- **Challenge Without Overwhelm:**
    Stretch goals are great—as long as they don't stretch your team into snapping.
    - Example: Set a baseline of 10 meetings/month, with a stretch goal of 12-15. Reward the overachievers with something meaningful, like public recognition or even chocolate (bribery works).

Chapter 2: Setting Targets and KPIs

- **Personalized Incentives:**
  Remember, your team is made up of individuals, not quota-bots. Tie quotas to what motivates each person.
  - Example: For a BDR eyeing a promotion, offer mentorship with a senior leader as a reward for exceeding quota by 110%. For someone who just survived 200 cold calls in a day, maybe send them a coffee—stat.
- **Gamification:**
  Quotas can feel heavy—why not make them fun?
  - Example: Launch a "Book 5 Meetings by Friday" challenge. First one to hit it gets a gift card, and everyone else gets the joy of knowing they tried.
- **Breaking Down Progress:**
  Monthly goals can feel like climbing Everest. Weekly milestones? More like hiking a nice trail with snacks.
  - Example: Instead of "Book 10 meetings by the end of the month," try "Book 2-3 meetings per week." Small wins keep morale high.

- **Blending Art and Science**

Scenario: You're entering a new vertical with longer sales cycles and higher deal values.
- **The Science:** Data shows you'll need 6 decision-maker meetings per month to hit your $200K pipeline goal.
- **The Art:** Frame the mission as an adventure into uncharted territory. Offer a reward for the most creative outreach that secures a high-profile account. Who doesn't love a little Indiana Jones moment in sales?

This balance of structure and inspiration ensures your team stays focused and energized—even when the going gets tough.

Quota Evolution: From Meetings to Revenue

Quotas should grow up with your team:
1. Phase 1: Focus on activity metrics like calls and emails to build habits.
2. Phase 2: Shift to pipeline contribution, emphasizing quality over quantity.
3. Phase 3: Tie quotas directly to revenue impact.

Example: A mature team might have quotas like generating $250K in pipeline per quarter, with bonuses tied to closed revenue.

Why This Matters

Quotas are more than just targets, they're a cultural statement. When done right:
- They celebrate progress, not just perfection.
- Foster creativity by rewarding out-of-the-box thinking.
- Align individual effort with team success, reminding everyone why they showed up in the first place.

When quotas strike the perfect balance of art and science, they inspire action, ignite innovation, and keep your team motivated to deliver results—without sacrificing their sanity.

Chapter 2: Setting Targets and KPIs

Balancing Individual and Team Success

Creating harmony between individual and team goals is critical to building a cohesive, high-performing BDR team. When done right, this balance not only drives results but also fosters accountability, collaboration, and shared ownership. Achieving this equilibrium requires a mix of strategic goal setting, intentional leadership, and a clear understanding of what motivates both individuals and teams.

The Psychology Behind Balancing Goals
Balancing individual and team goals taps into two powerful psychological drivers:
- **The Need for Autonomy:**
  Individual targets provide a sense of ownership. BDRs understand their specific contributions, which fosters accountability and pride.
  - Example: "Your 53 meetings directly contribute $200K in pipeline toward our $10M revenue target."
- **The Desire for Belonging:**
  Team goals fulfill the human need to be part of something bigger. When BDRs see how their efforts align with team success, they're motivated to go the extra mile for both themselves and their peers.

How It Works in Practice
The Waterfall Approach is an effective method for balancing individual and team objectives. By cascading large goals into smaller, actionable targets, it provides clarity at every level:
- **Clarity at All Levels:**
  Every BDR understands exactly how their work impacts team and company success.
  - Example: "If each BDR books 53 meetings this month, we'll hit our quarterly team goal of 1,600 meetings and ensure a healthy pipeline."
- **Avoiding Bottlenecks:**
  Breaking large goals into smaller targets helps identify bottlenecks early.
  - Example: If the team struggles to hit their monthly meeting quota, leaders can adjust strategies before it impacts the pipeline goal.
- **Promoting Collaboration:**
  Team targets encourage collaboration. BDRs share best practices, troubleshoot challenges together, and celebrate collective wins.
  - Example: Weekly brainstorming sessions on messaging can lead to higher response rates for everyone.
- **Driving Strategic Focus:**
  Individual targets align with larger business goals, ensuring every activity has a purpose.
  - Example: For enterprise-focused teams, quotas emphasize quality meetings with decision-makers over volume-driven metrics.

Chapter 2: Setting Targets and KPIs

Encouraging Collaboration Without Losing Accountability
Balancing individual accountability with team collaboration creates a win-win dynamic.

- **Collaboration Drives Innovation:**
  Sharing ideas and best practices leads to creative solutions.
  - Example: One team member experimenting with humor in emails increases response rates and inspires others to try similar approaches.
- **Accountability Drives Ownership:**
  Individual accountability ensures no one hides behind the group. Each BDR takes responsibility for their results.
- **Together, They Build Resilience:**
  Collaboration provides support during tough times, while accountability ensures challenges are faced head-on.

Avoiding Common Pitfalls
- **The "Free-Rider" Problem:**
  Without individual accountability, weaker performers can ride on the coattails of stronger teammates. Clear personal targets prevent this.
- **Toxic Competition:**
  Overemphasis on individual performance can breed unhealthy competition. Encouraging knowledge-sharing and recognizing collaboration reduces this risk.
- **Overwhelming Teamwork:**
  Excessive focus on collaboration can detract from individual productivity. Schedule collaborative activities at regular, manageable intervals.

The Bigger Picture
Balancing individual and team goals creates alignment at every level. It ensures that:
- BDRs feel personally responsible for their contributions.
- Teams work collaboratively to overcome challenges and share best practices.
- Leaders have visibility into team dynamics, allowing for proactive adjustments.

In the long run, this balance drives not just revenue but also culture. It fosters a team where:
- Individual wins are celebrated.
- Collaboration becomes second nature.
- Everyone is invested in a shared mission.

Chapter 2: Setting Targets and KPIs

Adjusting Targets for Changing Realities

The sales world is anything but static. Market conditions shift, prospects' priorities change, and even your product might evolve. In this unpredictable landscape, the ability to adjust targets flexibly is not a luxury—it's a necessity. Adjusting targets for changing realities ensures your team remains focused, motivated, and aligned with organizational goals, no matter the circumstances.

How to Adjust Targets Without Losing Direction

- **Collaborate with Frontline Teams**
  Your BDRs and Account Executives are closest to the action. Their insights provide critical context for setting realistic targets.
    - Ask questions like:
        - How long does it take to engage a prospect?
        - What outreach methods are resonating most?
        - What's a reasonable expectation for meetings booked in a week?

  Example: A BDR team noticed that email open rates plummeted after a competitor's price drop. The leader adjusted outreach strategies to focus on personalized LinkedIn messages, which yielded higher engagement.

- **Use Leading Indicators as Proxies**
  If outcomes (like closed revenue) are uncertain, focus on activities BDRs can control:
    - **Metrics to Monitor:**
        - Calls made, emails sent, or LinkedIn connections requested.
        - Time-to-follow-up or response rates for efficiency tracking.

  Over time, track how these activities correlate with outcomes, refining targets accordingly.

- **Set Short-Term Goals**
  Shorter goal cycles provide agility, letting you adapt quickly as you gather data.
    - Example:
        - Month 1: "Book 5 meetings per BDR while testing personalized messaging."
        - Month 2: "Increase to 8 meetings per BDR now that messaging is optimized."

  This approach keeps goals attainable while maintaining momentum.

- **Build in Buffer Zones**
  Introduce tiered targets to accommodate market uncertainty:
    - Base Target: Minimally acceptable performance.
    - Stretch Target: Challenging yet achievable goals.

  Example: Base: 6 meetings/month. Stretch: 10 meetings/month. High performers have something to push for, while under performers remain motivated.

Chapter 2: Setting Targets and KPIs

- **Trust the Power of Patterns**
  Even in volatile markets, patterns emerge if you're measuring the right things. Within 30–60 days, consistent trends will appear in metrics like call-to-meeting ratios or pipeline value generated per BDR. Use these trends as the foundation for refining future targets.

Why Flexibility is Your Greatest Asset

Rigid quotas built on outdated assumptions demotivate your team and miss opportunities for growth. Flexibility ensures targets evolve with your data, market, and team dynamics.

- **Proactive Iteration:**
  Leaders who adjust targets regularly prevent burnout, improve engagement, and keep their team aligned with shifting business objectives.

  Example: During a market downturn, a SaaS company reduced their monthly meeting quota by 20% but increased their focus on converting high-value accounts. This pivot resulted in a 15% pipeline growth despite fewer overall meetings.

Take-aways for a Balanced Approach
Adjusting targets isn't about chasing perfection—it's about maintaining progress. Combine:
- Insights from your team.
- Industry benchmarks.
- Real-time data.

This ensures targets are achievable, relevant, and motivational. Ultimately, your ability to adapt reinforces your team's trust in leadership while driving long-term success.

Chapter 3: Headcount Planning

Determining Team Size and Structure

Sizing your BDR team isn't a matter of gut instinct or "let's just add three more reps and see what happens." It's about crafting a well-oiled machine that drives pipeline and aligns perfectly with your revenue goals, sales process, and market dynamics. Get it wrong, and you'll have either overwhelmed reps burning out or underworked reps building elaborate Slack emojis. Get it right, and every seat in the team becomes a powerhouse of productivity.

Start with Reverse-Engineering Your Goals

If you're not working backward from your revenue targets, you're flying blind. Start with your company's revenue goals and break them into actionable pieces.

1. **Revenue Target → Deals Closed**
   - Divide your revenue target by the average deal size.
   - Example: A $10M quarterly goal with a $50K average deal size means 200 deals need to close.
2. **Deals Closed → Qualified Opportunities**
   - Multiply deals needed by the close rate.
   - Example: A 25% close rate means you'll need 800 qualified opportunities to close those 200 deals.
3. **Qualified Opportunities → Meetings Booked**
   - Divide by the meeting-to-opportunity conversion rate.
   - Example: If 50% of meetings convert, you'll need 1,600 meetings booked.
4. **Meetings Booked → Calls Made**
   - Factor in your calls-to-meeting ratio.
   - Example: If 10% of calls result in meetings, you'll need 16,000 calls.

Now, divide those calls across your BDRs.

If one BDR averages 1,000 calls/month, you'll need at least 16 BDRs to meet your goals—or rethink the ratio by adding new tools, better scripts, or a larger team.

Separate Inbound and Outbound Teams

Inbound and outbound BDRs are as different as sprinters and marathon runners. Sure, they're both "running," but the strategies, stamina, and skills required couldn't be more distinct.

- **Inbound SDRs:** Handle warm leads—prospects already familiar with your brand. They qualify, nurture, and route these leads to AEs.
- **Outbound BDRs:** Build pipeline from scratch. They target cold prospects, creating demand where none exists.

Pro Tip: Keep these roles separate. An inbound SDR juggling outbound targets will either ignore warm leads or burn out trying to do it all. Specialization ensures both roles get the focus they need.

Chapter 3: Headcount Planning

BDR-to-AE Ratios: A Delicate Balance
The ratio of BDRs to AEs can make or break your pipeline efficiency. Too many BDRs, and AEs are buried in unqualified leads. Too few, and AEs waste time prospecting instead of closing deals.

Benchmarks to Guide Your Ratio:
- 1:1 Ratio: Works for high-touch enterprise sales where each lead is heavily researched and nurtured.
- 2:1 Ratio: Ideal for mid-market teams that balance personalization with a need for scale.
- 3:1 or Higher: Perfect for high-volume, transactional sales models targeting SMBs.

Reality Check: If you're consistently missing pipeline targets, your ratio is probably off. A SaaS company that transitioned from a 1:1 to a 2:1 ratio saw a 25% increase in closed deals, as AEs focused on closing while BDRs fed them higher-quality leads.

Specialization: The Secret Sauce
Specialization within your BDR team isn't just a fancy buzzword—it's a proven way to increase efficiency and results.
- Market-Based: Assign reps to SMB, mid-market, or enterprise accounts.
- Industry-Based: Focus on specific verticals like healthcare, finance, or tech.
- Geographic-Based: Align reps with time zones and regional nuances to improve response times and rapport.

Example: A SaaS company targeting enterprise healthcare accounts found that industry-specialized BDRs booked 30% more meetings. They developed deeper knowledge of the vertical, spoke the prospect's language, and built credibility faster than generalists could.

Accounting for Growth and Seasonality
- **Scaling for Growth:**
  As your company scales, your BDR team should grow proportionally with lead volume. If pipeline goals are increasing by 20%, your team size (or productivity) needs to scale accordingly.

- **Seasonality:**
  Some industries experience peaks and valleys. For example:
  - A company selling HR software might see a surge in Q4 as budgets open.
  - A fitness platform might peak in Q1, riding the wave of New Year's resolutions.

Plan for temporary hires or workload adjustments during these times to prevent burnout and capitalize on demand spikes.

Determining Team Size and Structure

Chapter 3: Headcount Planning

When to Reevaluate Team Size
- Pipeline Stalls: If deals are drying up, it might indicate that your BDR team is stretched too thin.
- Lead Overload: If AEs are overwhelmed with leads but closing rates are slipping, you may need more BDRs to improve lead quality.
- Market Changes: A new competitor or shift in buyer priorities could mean reevaluating productivity metrics.

BDR Leadership Structure: When to Scale Leadership

Building a thriving BDR team isn't just about adding reps—it's about knowing when to add layers of leadership to ensure productivity, accountability, and career development. A well-timed investment in BDR leadership can make the difference between a high-performing team and one that feels chaotic or unsupported.

When to Add the Next Leadership Layer
Bringing in additional leadership should align with three critical milestones:
- **Team Size Growth**
  - The tipping point often comes when a single leader can no longer provide the hands-on coaching, oversight, and strategy alignment needed to maintain performance.
  - Guideline: Once you have more than 8–10 BDRs per manager, it's time to consider adding another layer. Beyond this, coaching quality declines, and reps can feel neglected.
- **Performance Plateaus**
  - If performance metrics stagnate despite team expansion, it may indicate a lack of one-on-one support or role clarity. Adding team leads or managers can reignite growth.
- **Career Pathing**
  - When senior BDRs begin seeking career progression within the team, creating leadership roles like team leads or associate managers offers a clear pathway while spreading the workload.

Wrapping It Up
Determining the size and structure of your BDR team isn't a one-and-done decision. It's a process of constant recalibration, guided by metrics, feedback, and a clear understanding of your business goals.

The right team isn't just big enough—it's specialized, efficient, and adaptable, ready to pivot with changing market realities while driving consistent pipeline growth.

Adjusting Targets for Changing Realities

Chapter 3: Headcount Planning

The Ideal Manager-to-Rep Ratio

The golden rule for BDR leadership is maintaining a manageable manager-to-rep ratio. Here are typical benchmarks:

- **Small Teams (1–5 BDRs)**
    - Manager-to-Rep Ratio: 1:5 or less.
    - Why: Smaller teams thrive under highly personalized coaching and mentorship.
- **Growing Teams (6–12 BDRs)**
    - Manager-to-Rep Ratio: 1:8 is optimal.
    - Why: This ensures managers can still provide one-on-one coaching while overseeing day-to-day team operations.
- **Large Teams (12+ BDRs)**
    - Solution: Introduce team leads or associate managers.
    - Why: Breaking the team into smaller pods (e.g., 6 reps per team lead) ensures continued support without overwhelming senior managers.

Signs You Need More Leadership
How do you know it's time to scale your leadership structure? Look for these signs:
- **Manager Burnout:**
    - A single manager juggling 15+ direct reports is stretched too thin, compromising both their ability to coach and their mental health.
- **Reps Lacking Support:**
    - If BDRs struggle with unanswered questions, inconsistent feedback, or unclear expectations, it's a sign the team has outgrown its leadership capacity.
- **Quality Drop:**
    - When outreach quality or pipeline contributions decline despite high activity levels, it may be due to a lack of coaching bandwidth.
- **Promotion Pipeline:**
    - As BDRs mature in their roles, some will naturally seek leadership opportunities. Adding team leads allows you to retain talent while fostering growth.

How to Build the Next Layer
- **Introduce Team Leads:**
    - Promote high-performing senior BDRs into team lead roles.
    - Responsibilities include mentoring new reps, overseeing daily activities, and bridging communication between reps and managers.
- **Add a Layer of Managers:**
    - For larger teams (15+ BDRs), create a second layer of managers overseeing multiple team leads. This ensures a balance of strategic oversight and hands-on support.

Chapter 3: Headcount Planning

- **Create Specialization:**
    - Assign leaders to specific groups (e.g., inbound vs. outbound, enterprise vs. SMB). This structure allows leaders to focus on the unique challenges and opportunities of their segment.

The Impact of Leadership Scaling
- Enhanced Coaching Quality:
    - With fewer direct reports, managers can provide personalized feedback and development plans.
- Increased Retention:
    - Clear career paths and adequate support lead to higher employee satisfaction and lower turnover.
- Sustainable Growth:
    - Scaling leadership ensures the team can grow without sacrificing quality or burning out existing managers.
- Faster Onboarding:
    - Team leads or additional managers can absorb the extra workload of training and onboarding new hires, reducing ramp-up time.

Real-World Example
A SaaS company scaled its BDR team from 8 to 25 reps within a year. Initially, one manager oversaw the entire team, but performance plateaued, and burnout became a problem. Introducing 3 team leads (each managing 6–8 reps) restored focus, and overall pipeline contributions increased by 30% in just 3 months.

Chapter 3: Headcount Planning

BDR-to-AE Ratios That Work

The BDR-to-AE ratio is a balancing act that affects how smoothly leads flow through your pipeline and, just as importantly, how effectively BDRs and AEs collaborate. At its core, this ratio defines not only the workload but also the working relationship between BDRs and AEs. Different ratios require different dynamics, and recognizing this is key to creating a harmonious and productive team.

The Impact of Ratios on Relationships

The BDR-to-AE ratio isn't just about numbers—it shapes how BDRs and AEs interact, how responsibilities are divided, and how they align toward shared goals.

- Low Ratios (1:1) foster deep, personalized collaboration, with BDRs and AEs essentially functioning as a unit.
- Medium Ratios (2:1) require a balance between close teamwork and operational independence.
- High Ratios (3:1 or more) push BDRs to operate with greater autonomy, feeding AEs a consistent pipeline with minimal back-and-forth.

Each setup has unique challenges and opportunities.

Exploring Common Ratios and Their Dynamics

1:1 Ratio – The Partnership Model
- Who It's For: Enterprise teams with complex sales cycles and high-value deals.
- How It Works: One BDR is dedicated to one AE, building a highly personalized and strategic approach to pipeline generation.

Relationship Dynamics:
- BDR Role: Acts as an extension of the AE, tailoring outreach and qualifying leads with precision.
- AE Role: Collaborates closely with the BDR, providing detailed input on target accounts and strategic priorities.
- Collaboration Style: Daily check-ins to discuss target accounts, review lead progress, and refine strategies.

Example: A BDR at an enterprise SaaS company spends a week researching a single account, identifying key stakeholders, and crafting custom messaging. The AE, armed with this detailed intel, conducts a high-stakes meeting that moves the account directly into a pilot phase.

2:1 Ratio – The Balanced Collaboration
- Who It's For: Mid-market teams balancing personalized outreach with scalability.

Chapter 3: Headcount Planning

- How It Works: Two BDRs feed a single AE, maintaining a steady flow of leads while still allowing for tailored approaches.

Relationship Dynamics:
- BDR Role: Focuses on generating a balanced mix of volume and quality, splitting time between deep account research and broader outreach efforts.
- AE Role: Works with both BDRs to prioritize accounts and manage follow-ups, offering occasional coaching to align messaging.
- Collaboration Style: Weekly syncs to set priorities and review account progress, with BDRs leveraging insights from the AE to refine their outreach.

Example: A cybersecurity startup's AE holds a Monday meeting with their two BDRs to align on the week's priorities. One BDR focuses on dormant accounts, while the other targets new prospects. This division of labor ensures no leads fall through the cracks.

3:1 Ratio (or Higher) – The Independent Pipeline Machine
- Who It's For: SMB teams with high-volume, transactional sales models.
- How It Works: Three or more BDRs generate a high volume of opportunities for a single AE, emphasizing speed and efficiency over deep account engagement.

Relationship Dynamics:
- BDR Role: Operates with greater autonomy, focusing on activity-driven metrics like calls made or emails sent to generate leads en masse.
- AE Role: Primarily responsible for qualifying and closing leads, with minimal input on the initial outreach process.
- Collaboration Style: Light-touch communication, typically focused on lead handoff and pipeline updates.

Example: A fitness tech company uses a 3:1 ratio to handle SMB sales. BDRs follow a set cadence to qualify leads quickly, handing off opportunities to an AE who moves them through a streamlined close process.

Adapting Your Approach for Each Ratio

Low Ratios (1:1)
- Strengths: Deep alignment and high-quality pipeline generation.
- Challenges: Requires significant input from AEs, which can slow the process.
- Leadership Focus: Encourage consistent communication and shared accountability between BDRs and AEs.

Chapter 3: Headcount Planning

Medium Ratios (2:1)
- Strengths: Strikes a balance between scalability and collaboration.
- Challenges: Requires clear role boundaries to avoid duplication of effort.
- Leadership Focus: Provide structured workflows and clear priorities to prevent BDRs from competing for the AE's attention.

High Ratios (3:1 or Higher)
- Strengths: Maximizes activity and pipeline volume.
- Challenges: Risk of misalignment or lead bottlenecks without strong processes.
- Leadership Focus: Emphasize autonomy for BDRs while maintaining clear handoff protocols to ensure leads are fully qualified.

Finding Your Team's Sweet Spot
Ratios aren't static—they evolve as your team grows and your market shifts. To find the ideal balance:
1. Start with Benchmarks: Use industry norms as a starting point, but tailor ratios to your business needs.
2. Monitor Relationships: Regularly check in with BDRs and AEs to ensure alignment, avoiding friction over lead quality or follow-up timing.
3. Iterate Based on Data: Use pipeline velocity and conversion metrics to refine your approach over time.

The Takeaway
The BDR-to-AE ratio isn't just about balancing numbers—it's about balancing relationships. When aligned, these ratios foster trust, efficiency, and collaboration between teams. Whether your focus is on deep partnerships, balanced collaboration, or high-volume independence, understanding how ratios shape dynamics is key to driving sustainable growth.

Chapter 3: Headcount Planning

Scaling for Growth (and Surviving It)

Scaling a BDR function is like trying to grow a garden in the middle of a windstorm. The goal is not just to plant seeds (BDRs) but to ensure each one thrives despite ever-changing conditions. Growth brings opportunities but also chaos. The secret is knowing how to expand without breaking the foundation you've built.

Why Scaling BDR Teams Feels Like a Balancing Act

1. Increased Complexity
   - As your team grows, so do the layers of processes, personalities, and challenges. What worked for a 5-person team may crumble under the weight of a 25-person department.
2. Resource Strain
   - Tools, management, and onboarding systems that supported your smaller team may start to falter.
3. Market Dynamics
   - Entering new verticals or scaling outreach efforts demands flexibility in how your team operates.

Example: When a SaaS company doubled its BDR headcount in six months, it discovered its old CRM system couldn't handle the increased activity. This resulted in missed follow-ups and duplicate outreach—undermining the very purpose of scaling.

Phases of Scaling

Phase 1: Establishing the Core
- Focus: Strong foundations are everything. This includes clear processes, playbooks, and metrics.
- Key Consideration: Before scaling, assess If your current team is hitting its stride. If performance is inconsistent, scaling amplifies these issues.

Phase 2: Scaling Teams
- Focus: Add headcount, but strategically. Avoid the temptation to flood the team with hires if your processes can't support them.
- Key Consideration: Break the team into pods (e.g., inbound/outbound or by geography) to manage growth effectively.

Phase 3: Refining Operations
- Focus: Streamline workflows, automate repetitive tasks, and fine-tune performance management.
- Key Consideration: Don't overcomplicate. Scaling shouldn't mean drowning in bureaucracy.

Chapter 3: Headcount Planning

Common Pitfalls and How to Avoid Them
- **Over-Hiring Before Readiness**
  - Trap: Bringing on too many BDRs before infrastructure is ready leads to confusion and inefficiency.
  - Solution: Start small, expand incrementally, and continuously reassess capacity.
- **Neglecting Leadership Needs**
  - Trap: A single manager overseeing 15+ reps is a recipe for burnout and poor coaching.
  - Solution: Introduce team leads or add management layers as your team grows past 8-10 reps per manager.
- **Ignoring Culture During Growth**
  - Trap: Rapid hiring can dilute your team's values and morale.
  - Solution: Codify and communicate your team's culture—then hire for cultural fit, not just skills.

Example: A fintech startup scaled from 6 to 18 BDRs in under a year but faced 30% turnover due to misaligned hires. Revamping their hiring process to prioritize adaptability and collaboration reduced churn by half the following year.

Leadership Strategies for Scaling
1. **Proactively Identify Bottlenecks**
   - Monitor KPIs like lead follow-up times and pipeline quality. Slippage in these areas often indicates growing pains.
2. **Empower Team Leads**
   - Promote top performers into mentorship or team lead roles to maintain coaching and morale without overloading managers.
3. **Keep Lines of Communication Open**
   - Regular check-ins and feedback loops ensure you catch small issues before they become systemic.

Final Thoughts
Scaling your BDR team is a marathon, not a sprint. It's about managing complexity without sacrificing culture, driving efficiency while maintaining quality, and adapting to growth without losing sight of your team's core purpose: fueling the pipeline with quality opportunities.

Chapter 3: Headcount Planning

Seasonal vs. Long-Term Needs

Planning for seasonal spikes and long-term growth in your BDR function requires more than just headcount adjustments. It's about creating a structure that thrives in both steady and fluctuating conditions, ensuring your team can meet short-term demands without sacrificing long-term sustainability.

Understanding Seasonal Needs

Some industries experience predictable demand fluctuations based on external factors:
- Retail Tech: Peaks during holiday shopping seasons.
- HR Software: Spikes in Q4 as companies set budgets or in Q1 during hiring pushes.
- Tax Solutions: Surge during tax season.

If you're not planning for these swings, you're setting up your team for either burnout during busy periods or underutilization during lulls.

Strategies for Managing Seasonal Spikes

1. Temporary Hiring:
   - Bring on temporary or contract BDRs to handle surges without committing to long-term headcount.
   - Example: A SaaS company specializing in e-commerce tools hired 5 seasonal BDRs each fall to handle increased demand. Their training focused on just the essentials to ramp them quickly.
2. Redistributing Workloads:
   - Shift focus among your team. During off-seasons, have BDRs focus on pipeline-building activities like prospect research or account mapping.
3. Optimizing Outreach Timing:
   - Tailor campaigns to align with high-response periods. Train your team to recognize when prospects are most likely to engage.

Planning for Long-Term Growth

While seasonal adjustments are reactive, long-term planning is proactive. As your business grows, your BDR function must evolve to keep pace with increased pipeline demands and organizational complexity.

Key Considerations for Sustainable Growth

- **Pipeline-to-Revenue Ratios:**
   - Align headcount and activity levels with revenue projections.
   - Example: If your revenue goal increases by 25%, your pipeline targets—and thus your BDR team's capacity—should scale proportionally.
- **Skill Development:**
   - Equip your team with skills for evolving challenges, such as selling to larger accounts or entering new markets.

Chapter 3: Headcount Planning

Budgeting for Team Expansion

Budgeting for a BDR team isn't a simple calculation of salaries and tools—it's a strategic exercise in resource allocation and long-term planning. Each decision directly impacts pipeline health, team morale, and revenue potential. Let's break this topic into actionable layers to ensure depth and precision.

Understanding the Full Cost of Expansion

Beyond Salaries
Expanding your team involves direct and indirect costs:

- **Compensation:**
  Base salary, bonuses, and commissions.
  Benchmarking against industry standards ensures you attract top talent.
    - Example: A mid-market SaaS company allocates $65K/year for base salary and $20K/year in bonuses for each BDR, ensuring competitiveness in a tight labor market.

- **Onboarding and Training:**
  Costs include both internal resources (managers' time, training materials) and third-party programs.
    - Example: If it takes 3 months to fully ramp a new hire at $6K/month salary, that's $18K before they contribute to the pipeline.

- **Tools and Tech Stack:**
    - CRM systems, engagement platforms, and analytics tools.
    - Real Numbers: A CRM license costs $100/user/month, and a prospecting tool adds $120/month. For a 10-person team, that's $26,400 annually.

- **Management Overhead:**
  As the team grows, so do leadership needs. Account for manager salaries and the cost of team leads if scaling past 8–10 BDRs.

- **Attrition and Replacement:**
  Include costs associated with hiring and training replacements due to natural turnover.
    - Estimate: Losing a BDR can cost up to $50K in productivity loss, hiring fees, and ramp time.

Projecting ROI for Expansion

To justify budgets, connect headcount increases to measurable outcomes.
- **Estimate Revenue Impact Per Hire:**
    - Calculate how much pipeline and revenue each BDR contributes annually.
    - Example: A BDR generates $1.2M in pipeline annually with a 10% close rate, resulting in $120K of closed revenue.

Chapter 3: Headcount Planning

- **Tie Revenue Goals to Headcount Needs:**
    - Work backward from the revenue goal to determine how many BDRs are required.
    - Example: For a $10M revenue target, requiring $50M in pipeline at a 20% close rate, you'd need approximately 42 BDRs generating $1.2M each.
- **Account for Non-Revenue Activities:**
    - BDRs also handle prospecting, nurturing, and account research, which indirectly influence deal velocity and win rates.

Building a Scalable Budget Framework

A flexible framework ensures you can adapt to market shifts or unexpected changes:
- Fixed Costs:
    - Management salaries, office space, and core tools remain constant as headcount grows.
- Variable Costs:
    - Scale based on the number of reps. This includes bonuses, new software licenses, and incremental training costs.
- Forecast Buffers:
    - Include contingency funds for unexpected hiring surges, tool upgrades, or market shifts.
    - Tip: Allocate 10–15% of your BDR budget as a buffer.

Aligning Budgets with Business Phases

The needs of your BDR team evolve depending on your company's growth stage:
- **Startup Phase**
    - Focus: Prove the sales model.
    - Budget Priorities: Small, scrappy team with investments in versatile tools and aggressive onboarding.
- **Scaling Phase**
    - Focus: Expand into new markets or verticals.
    - Budget Priorities: Increased headcount and specialized leadership roles (team leads, dedicated managers).
- **Mature Phase**
    - Focus: Optimize efficiency and expand revenue streams.
    - Budget Priorities: Advanced tools (e.g., intent data platforms) and a focus on reducing churn costs.

Managing Stakeholder Buy-In

Securing budget approval requires framing the investment as critical to achieving broader business goals.
- **Revenue Alignment:**
    - Present headcount growth as a necessary driver for meeting pipeline and revenue targets.

Budgeting for Team Expansion

Chapter 3: Headcount Planning

- **Efficiency Metrics:**
  - Show how BDR expansion reduces cost-per-qualified-opportunity or improves pipeline velocity.
- **Risk Mitigation:**
  - Highlight the risks of underinvestment, such as overburdening current reps or missing market opportunities.

Case Study: From Budget to Execution
A Fintech Company's Growth Journey

Stage 1: Initial Team of 5 BDRs
- Generated $500K pipeline/month ($100K/rep).
- Focused on SMB accounts with a 1:2 ratio of AEs to BDRs.

Challenge: Company entered mid-market sales, requiring deeper account research and higher lead quality.

Solution:
- Added 10 more BDRs, focusing on enterprise and mid-market accounts.
- Introduced team leads to manage pods of 7 reps.
- Budget: $800K for salaries, $50K for onboarding/training, and $30K for incremental tech stack upgrades.

Outcome: Within 6 months, the team increased pipeline contributions by 60%, driving an additional $8M in annual revenue.

Key Takeaways
1. Budget Beyond Salaries: Consider onboarding, tools, and management as part of the equation.
2. Model ROI Clearly: Align headcount increases with revenue impact to make a strong business case.
3. Build Flexibility: Scale incrementally, with room for adjustments based on real-time data and market needs.

Chapter 4: What to Expect of BDRs

A Day in the Life of a BDR

Being a BDR is like starring in your own action movie every day. There's strategy, a little chaos, some adrenaline-filled outreach, and (hopefully) a satisfying resolution. The key to making it all work? A day that's structured but leaves room for creativity and quick pivots when something unexpected happens—like a prospect actually answering their phone.

Focused Preparation and Strategy

This is the pre-game warmup. Before a single email is sent or call is made, a solid plan keeps the day from turning into a whirlwind of random activities.

- **Team Huddle or Stand-Up**
  Think of this as a locker room pep talk. It's where the team shares quick wins ("I booked a meeting with a GIF of a dancing dog") and discusses strategy for the day. Energy is contagious, and nothing sets the tone better than a quick dose of team spirit.
- **Research and Targeting**
  This is Sherlock Holmes mode: gathering clues, understanding your prospects, and figuring out what makes them tick. It's not just LinkedIn stalking (though that's part of it). It's spotting trends like, "Oh, they just raised Series C funding. Let me position this as helping them scale."
- **Sync with AEs**
  This is where the magic of teamwork happens. AEs bring insights about deal flow; BDRs bring the groundwork. Together, they plot how to storm the castle (aka close big deals).
- **Discovery Calls**
  This isn't about rattling off a checklist of qualifying questions. It's about listening and empathizing: "You've been trying to scale customer onboarding? Tell me more." When they open up, you know you're doing it right.
- **Demo Calls**
  Demos are like movie trailers—give them just enough to get excited, but don't spoil the whole plot. Leave them thinking, "I need to see how this ends."
- **Cold Outreach, BDR Edition**
  Sending out emails that say, "Just circling back" isn't outreach; it's inbox clutter. Modern outreach is personal, engaging, and maybe a little quirky.
  - Example: "Hey [Name], saw your company is hiring like crazy—growth pains, huh? We've helped companies like yours keep scaling pain-free. Got 15 minutes?"
- **Multi-Channel Engagement**
  - Email and calls are just the start. Modern BDRs engage across:
  - LinkedIn comments to casually enter a prospect's radar.
  - Direct video messages via Vidyard or Loom to humanize the pitch.
- **Follow-Ups That Feel Less... Follow-Up-y**
  Instead of "Just checking in." try to offer value:"Hey [Name], saw this article about [industry trend]. Thought it might resonate based on our last convo!"

Chapter 4: What to Expect of BDRs

- **Intelligent Follow-Ups**
  Instead of generic check-ins, BDRs follow up with something new—like a relevant industry stat, competitor analysis, or a personalized video addressing an earlier objection.
  Example, nobody likes, "Just checking in." Instead, offer value: "Hey [Name], saw this article about [industry trend]. Thought it might resonate based on our last convo!"

Creative and Reflection Time
This is the "thinking outside the box" part of the day—the time when you let loose, experiment, and maybe surprise yourself.
- **Creative Outreach Experiments**
  Ever tried sending a prospect a meme about their industry pain points? Or maybe a "prospect survival kit" with coffee and a stress ball? These aren't gimmicks—they're icebreakers that get noticed.
  - Example: One BDR sent a prospect a playlist called "Songs for Scaling a SaaS Company." The prospect replied: "This is genius. Let's talk."
- **Reflection: Learn, Don't Just Log**
  Instead of just ticking boxes in the CRM, think: "What worked today? What felt flat? What patterns am I seeing?" Some of the best ideas come from connecting the dots during quiet moments.

Collaboration and Refinement
Sharpen the axe. This part of the day is about making tomorrow's outreach even better.
- **Call Reviews That Don't Feel Painful**
  Nobody likes listening to their own voice, but these sessions aren't about nitpicking—they're about spotting hidden gems. Maybe you nailed an objection or found a phrase that really resonated. Bank it for future use.
- **Stealing Ideas from the Team**
  Okay, it's technically "collaborating." But let's be real: someone on your team probably cracked a tricky persona last week. Why reinvent the wheel when you can just learn from their brilliance?

Reflection and Forward Planning
End your day with purpose. Don't just slam your laptop shut—set yourself up for success tomorrow.
- **CRM Hygiene Is Self-Care**
  Yes, it's boring, but future you will thank current you for keeping notes detailed and accurate. Nobody wants to look at an old lead and think, "What even happened here?"
- **Plan Like a Boss**
  Look at tomorrow's targets, block time for high-priority accounts, and prep your messaging. It's a productivity hack disguised as being organized.

Chapter 4: What to Expect of BDRs

- Accounts with high engagement get personalized follow-ups.
- Dormant leads are scheduled for reactivation campaigns.
- New tools or experiments are prepped for A/B testing.

The Rhythm of Success
A BDR's day is a mix of hustle, strategy, and creativity. When structured well, it's not just about hitting numbers—it's about making an impact, building relationships, and enjoying the process. Because let's face it: when you book that big meeting or crack a tough account, there's no better feeling.

Managers, Take Note: BDRs Wear Multiple Hats
BDRs aren't just "meeting bookers"—they're strategists, researchers, negotiators, and sometimes even therapists (because who else understands the pain of a cold email gone unanswered?). The role demands juggling priorities, shifting gears between creative outreach and analytical follow-ups, and collaborating with multiple stakeholders, all while staying laser-focused on pipeline goals.

As a manager, understanding these nuances is critical. Your BDRs are:
- Detectives: Uncovering prospect pain points and figuring out what makes them tick.
- Storytellers: Crafting narratives that connect a prospect's challenges to your solution.
- Relationship Builders: Fostering trust with AEs, marketing, and even operations to ensure smooth handoffs.
- Problem Solvers: Finding ways around objections, gatekeepers, and that one prospect who's been "checking their calendar" for three weeks.

When managers see the role through this multifaceted lens, they can better support their BDRs with tailored coaching, realistic expectations, and encouragement to thrive—not just survive—in the role.

Chapter 4: What to Expect of BDRs

Weekly Routines for Success

A week in the life of a BDR isn't just about hammering out calls or flooding inboxes. It's about finding a rhythm—a mix of focus, creativity, and collaboration. The right weekly routine balances grind with growth, making every day feel purposeful while keeping the team energized.

Here's how to turn a week into a masterpiece.
Monday: Align and Activate
Mondays are about setting the tone, shaking off the weekend cobwebs, and diving into the week with focus and optimism (and, let's be real, a lot of coffee).

- **Kickoff Meeting**
  This isn't just a rehash of last week's numbers; it's a pep rally disguised as strategy. Start with a quick success story from the team, followed by clear goals for the week. A sprinkle of humor or a motivational meme doesn't hurt.
    - Example: A BDR shares how they booked a meeting with a prospect who responded to a cleverly personalized Spotify playlist titled "Songs for Scaling a SaaS Company."
- **Pipeline Prioritization**
- Identify accounts or prospects that need attention immediately—like the lead who just downloaded three whitepapers at 2 a.m. (hot lead alert!)
- **Motivation Starter**
- Share something to energize the team: a quick anecdote, a quirky sales tip, or even a friendly competition for the week (e.g., "First person to book five meetings gets a coffee delivered to their desk!").

Tuesday: Deep Work, Deep Wins
Tuesday is the unsung hero of the week—it's when the real work gets done. No frills, just focused execution.

- **Hyper-Personalized Outreach**
  This is where BDRs dig into their creativity vault. It's not about sending 100 emails; it's about sending 10 emails so specific the prospect can't help but reply.
    - Example: A BDR crafts a video pitch tailored to a CFO, referencing the company's recent earnings call and how their solution aligns with a stated growth priority.
- **1:1 Coaching**
  Managers hold short sessions to address specific challenges: a stuck deal, a low-performing campaign, or that one prospect who keeps ghosting. These aren't lectures—they're problem-solving brainstorms.

Wednesday: Midweek Calibration
Wednesdays are the week's pivot point. If something's not working, it's time to fix it. If everything's firing on all cylinders, it's time to double down.

- **Team Workshop**
Host a training on a hot topic, like new ways to crack gatekeepers or how to inject humor into outreach without sounding like a stand-up comic. Bring in a

Chapter 4: What to Expect of BDRs

top-performing AE or even a guest speaker to keep things fresh.
  - Tip: Gamify the session—run a mini roleplay competition with a small prize for the "Best Objection Smasher."
- **Creative Problem-Solving**
  Gather the team for a quick brainstorm on a shared challenge. Maybe response rates are dipping, or a competitor's undercutting pricing. Let the team riff on creative solutions, like themed email campaigns or unexpected outreach tactics (hello, snail mail care packages).

Thursday: Relationship Building Day
By Thursday, outreach is in full swing, but it's also time to focus on the people around you—AEs, prospects, and teammates. Relationships drive results.
- **AE Sync**
  These aren't just status updates—they're mini-strategy sessions. BDRs share what they've learned from their outreach, while AEs give context on which accounts need extra attention. Bonus points if someone brings donuts.
- **Peer Coaching**
  Pair up BDRs to review each other's calls, emails, or LinkedIn messages. Peer-to-peer feedback can uncover blind spots managers might miss.

Friday: Wrap and Reflect
Fridays are about tying everything together, celebrating the wins, and learning from the misses. Think of it as the season finale of your week—you want it to end on a high note.
- **Wins and Learnings Meeting**
  Every BDR shares one win and one insight from the week. It could be a creative outreach that worked, a new objection-handling trick, or even a funny fail that became a learning moment.
  - Example: A BDR shares how their prospect finally responded after three weeks of silence—turns out the prospect loved the BDR's humorous follow-up subject line: "Did my email get lost in your inbox's Bermuda Triangle?"
- **Pipeline Review**
  Take stock of where things stand. Which leads are progressing? Which need more attention next week? Leave no stone unturned before heading into the weekend.
- **Celebrate Like You Mean It**
  Recognition doesn't have to be grand—sometimes, a shoutout during the team meeting or a small reward for hitting a goal can make all the difference. (But if someone hit a major milestone, maybe it's time to bust out the pizza budget.)

Chapter 4: What to Expect of BDRs

Why Weekly Routines Matter
Weekly routines don't just organize work—they give it meaning. They create a cadence where BDRs know what to expect, when to push, and when to pause. The best routines:
- Balance structure with flexibility.
- Keep things fresh through creativity and collaboration.
- Focus on progress, not just activity.

With a rhythm like this, every week becomes an opportunity to grow—not just in numbers, but as a team.

Why Starting the Week Strong Matters
A strong Monday sets the tone for everything that follows. Momentum isn't something you stumble into; it's something you build. When a team kicks off the week with energy and clarity, it creates a ripple effect that boosts focus and productivity all week long.
- Psychology of a Fresh Start: Mondays are when most people feel the drive to get organized and tackle their to-do lists. Prospects are setting their priorities, which makes it the perfect time to position your outreach as the solution to their top challenges.
- Team Energy is Contagious: A motivated team on Monday morning carries that energy into their outreach. Success is fueled by enthusiasm, and nothing dampens enthusiasm like a sluggish start.

The Underrated Power of Friday Evenings
Fridays often get dismissed as "dead zones" for outreach, but they hold hidden potential—especially in the evening.
- A Prospect's Mindset is Looser: By Friday evening, many prospects are shifting gears. They've cleared their high-priority tasks, the week's chaos has settled, and their guard is often down. This makes them more receptive to candid conversations.
- Standing Out When Others Stop: Many sales reps wind down their efforts by Friday afternoon, assuming prospects won't engage. That's your cue to stand out. A thoughtful message or a well-timed call during this window can grab attention when there's less competition.

Example: One BDR sent a prospect a humorous email at 5:30 PM on a Friday, referencing the weekend ahead: "Before you escape for the weekend, I thought I'd give you something exciting to think about for Monday—how we can help solve [specific challenge]. Let's connect next week!" The prospect replied within minutes and booked a meeting.

The Weekly Bookends Strategy
By combining a strong Monday kickoff with strategic Friday outreach, BDRs can maximize their week. Start with purpose and end with a flourish—because it's not about working harder, but smarter, where it counts.

Chapter 4: What to Expect of BDRs

Mastering the Monthly Rhythm: Avoiding End-of-Month Madness

Monthly goals can feel like a race, but when you pace yourself smartly, you avoid the frantic sprint at the finish line. A well-structured approach to the month—one that balances urgency with planning—can transform how BDRs operate. The secret? Going hard early in the month and using the latter half to set up the next month for success.

The Power of Front-Loading Effort

The start of the month is when the team should hit the ground running. Energy is high, the pressure is low (relatively speaking), and prospects haven't yet been inundated with end-of-month pitches from other sales teams.

- **Focus on Closing Early:**
  - The first two weeks are the perfect time to finalize meetings for the current month. Prospects are more receptive, especially after the dust has settled from their own end-of-month rush.
  - Prioritize warm leads and accounts close to booking meetings, giving you early wins that build confidence.
- **Why It Works:**
  - Knocking out a significant chunk of your meeting goal early reduces stress and creates momentum for the rest of the month.

The Mid-Month Transition

Once the month's meetings are largely secured, shift focus toward building the pipeline for the next month. This isn't just a time-management trick; it's about setting yourself (and your AEs) up for long-term success.

- **Schedule Ahead, Avoid Chaos:**
  - Start reaching out to prospects for next month's meetings while calendars are still relatively open. Prospects are more likely to commit to future dates when they aren't being bombarded with last-minute pitches.
- **Experiment with Timing and Messaging:**
  - With less pressure to book immediate meetings, test new outreach strategies. Whether it's personalized video messages or interactive polls on LinkedIn, this is your sandbox.

Avoiding the End-of-Month Scramble

When you don't pace the month well, the last week becomes a high-stakes scramble. Here's how front-loading helps you avoid the chaos:

1. **Predictable Pacing:**
   - A strong first half ensures you're on track for your goals, reducing the need for desperate measures in the final days.
2. **Less Desperation, More Strategy:**
   - When you're not racing against the clock, your outreach stays thoughtful and personalized instead of rushed and generic.
3. **Consistent Morale:**
   - Avoiding this frenzy prevents burnout and keeps the team motivated.

Chapter 4: What to Expect of BDRs

Building the Habit of Forward Momentum
The first-half/second-half strategy isn't just a tactical adjustment; it's a mindset shift. BDRs learn to work smarter, think ahead, and take control of their schedules instead of being controlled by deadlines.
- Tip for Managers: Reinforce this rhythm during monthly reviews. Celebrate early wins, and emphasize the importance of setting the next month up for success.

Example of a Balanced Month
- **Weeks 1–2:**
    - Close 70% of meetings for the current month.
    - Prioritize hot leads and engage prospects who've shown intent.
- **Weeks 3–4:**
    - Shift focus to scheduling next month's meetings.
    - Experiment with creative outreach to re-engage dormant leads or target new accounts.

The Payoff: No More Madness
With this approach, the end-of-month isn't a source of stress—it's a time to refine, reflect, and prepare for the next cycle. BDRs finish strong, not frazzled, with a pipeline that feels robust and a strategy that's sustainable.

Running a Review That Matters
The monthly review isn't a chore; it's a golden opportunity for growth, reflection, and alignment. Here's how to make it engaging and impactful:

Start with the Wins
Nobody likes a meeting that starts with, "So, what went wrong?" Celebrate what went right first. Whether it's someone who crushed their quota or an experimental outreach that worked wonders, highlight the victories.
- Example: A BDR shares how their creative video message landed them a meeting with an elusive enterprise account.

Dive Into the Data
Make the data work for you, not the other way around. Use your CRM and analytics tools to uncover patterns, trends, and areas for improvement.
- Discuss conversion rates at every stage: How many calls led to meetings? How many meetings progressed to opportunities?
- Segment data by account type or persona to identify trends.

Collaborative Problem-Solving
Turn challenges into opportunities by involving the team in solutions.
- Example: If response rates have dipped, brainstorm new approaches together, like testing different email subject lines or timing outreach for off-hours.

Chapter 4: What to Expect of BDRs

The Coaching Conversation
Monthly reviews aren't just about numbers—they're about growth. Use these sessions to focus on individual development.
- Tailored Feedback:
- Go beyond generic advice. Offer specific, actionable guidance like:
  - "Your emails are strong, but they could benefit from more urgency in the call-to-action."
- Future-Focused Coaching:
- Don't dwell on past misses—use them to set up future wins. Discuss how to apply lessons learned to next month's goals.

Chapter 4: What to Expect of BDRs

Creating Consistency Without Micromanaging

Let's face it: micromanaging is a lose-lose game. It makes managers look like helicopter parents and makes BDRs feel like their every move is under surveillance. The real secret to consistency isn't a 24/7 watchful eye; it's trust, accountability, and creating an environment where the team operates like a well-rehearsed jazz band—improvising within a structure but always in sync.

Trust: The Foundation of Consistency

Trust isn't something you sprinkle into a team meeting and hope it sticks. It's built through deliberate actions that show your team you believe in their abilities—and that you're here to support, not micromanage.

- **Start with Clarity**
  A confused BDR is an inconsistent BDR. From the very beginning, make expectations crystal clear:
  - What does success look like?
  - What are the must-hit metrics, and where's the room for flexibility?
  - What's the role of creativity versus process adherence?

  Example: "Our goal is 10 booked meetings a month per rep. How you get there—calls, emails, LinkedIn DMs, carrier pigeons—is up to you, as long as the meetings are solid."

- **Be Transparent Yourself**
  Your team will mirror your behavior. If you're open about challenges, decisions, and strategy pivots, BDRs will follow suit. Show them the "why" behind changes, whether it's adjusting a quota or shifting focus to a new vertical.

  Example: "We're moving priority to fintech accounts because we're seeing a 15% higher response rate in that segment."

Accountability: The Partner of Autonomy

Here's the thing: accountability doesn't mean finger-pointing. It's about creating a culture where BDRs own their results, celebrate their wins, and proactively address gaps.

- **Make Commitments Public**
  There's something magical about a BDR saying their goals out loud. Public commitments—whether in team meetings, Slack channels, or 1:1s—build a sense of shared accountability.

  Example: "This week, I'm focusing on five dormant accounts and booking at least three meetings from them."

- **Recognize the Process, Not Just the Results**
  Consistency isn't always about hitting the goal—it's about showing up, putting in the effort, and learning along the way. Highlight the BDR who tried three new outreach techniques, even if only one worked.

  Pro Tip: Celebrate process wins in team huddles. "Shoutout to Alex for testing a new subject line that increased open rates by 20%—let's all give it a shot!"

Chapter 4: What to Expect of BDRs

Empowerment: The Antidote to Micromanagement
The reason most managers micromanage? Fear. Fear that tasks won't get done, goals won't be hit, or reps will go rogue. But the cure for that fear isn't control—it's empowerment.

- **Let Them Experiment**
  Every BDR has their own style, and forcing everyone into the same mold kills creativity. Instead, encourage experimentation with outreach techniques, messaging, and engagement strategies.
  Example: A BDR who hates cold calls might thrive on LinkedIn. Let them focus on what works, as long as it drives results.
- **Provide Guardrails, Not Chains**
  Structure is important, but too much of it stifles initiative. Give your team a framework for success, but allow room for improvisation.
  Example: "Here's our standard cadence for cold outreach, but if you think you can rework it to hit your style, go for it. Let's review the results in a week."

Feedback Loops Instead of Checklists
If you're reviewing every email, call, and CRM note, you're not leading—you're babysitting. Consistency comes from feedback loops that teach BDRs how to self-correct and improve.

Use 1:1s Wisely
These aren't status updates—they're coaching sessions. Focus on skill-building, not micromanaging metrics.
- Example: "Your email subject lines are good, but they could be punchier. Let's brainstorm a few together."

Encourage Peer Reviews
BDRs often learn more from each other than from their managers. Build a culture of collaboration by encouraging reps to review each other's work.
- Example: "Pair up and exchange your top-performing email templates this week—then steal shamelessly."

Culture of Trust + Accountability = Consistency
When you foster a high-trust, high-accountability culture, consistency becomes a natural byproduct.

Managers: Step Back and Watch the Magic
Micromanaging robs your team of ownership, which is the backbone of consistency. Once trust is established, you'll notice:
- BDRs set higher standards for themselves.
- Goals are hit more often—without a manager hovering nearby.
- Creativity flourishes, leading to more effective outreach and stronger results.

Chapter 4: What to Expect of BDRs

A Real-World Example
At a tech startup, the sales manager replaced daily check-ins with weekly "progress showcases." Each BDR shared wins, learnings, and struggles, with minimal managerial intervention. Within three months, the team's meeting-to-opportunity conversion rate improved by 25%, simply because reps felt empowered to own their performance.

The Role of Culture in Consistency
Finally, consistency isn't just a process—it's part of your team's DNA. When BDRs feel they're part of a supportive, high-trust environment, they'll naturally align with expectations.
- Recognize and Reward: Celebrate consistency as much as big wins. A BDR who hits their goals every month deserves as much recognition as the one who books the occasional high-profile meeting.
- Promote Collaboration: Consistency improves when BDRs see themselves as part of a team with shared accountability, not as lone wolves.

Mastering Iteration: Making Continuous Improvement Part of Your DNA
Every great leader knows that iteration isn't a one-time thing—it's a mindset. It's about treating every win, loss, and hiccup as data for improvement. If your BDR team is going to thrive, continuous iteration must become part of their daily rhythm.

Here's how to weave iteration into your team's DNA:
1. Create a "Test and Learn" Culture
Encourage experimentation by framing every change as a test, not a final decision. Whether it's a new cadence or a fresh outreach tactic, emphasize that results—good or bad—are valuable learning moments.
- Example: "Let's A/B test these email openings for a week and see which one resonates better."

When failure is reframed as feedback, reps are more likely to innovate without fear of blame.

2. Document the Iterations
If it's not written down, it didn't happen. Every tweak, insight, and test result should be documented so the team can reference what's worked—and what hasn't.
- Use tools like Notion or Google Docs to build a shared knowledge base.
- Make it accessible, so team members can add their learnings in real time.

3. Keep Feedback Loops Short and Frequent
Quarterly reviews are great, but iteration happens in the day-to-day grind. Use weekly or bi-weekly check-ins to:
- Share insights from recent experiments.
- Highlight what's working and what needs refining.

Creating Consistency Without Micromanaging

Chapter 4: What to Expect of BDRs

- Encourage reps to voice their ideas for improvement.

4. Make It Fun
Turn iteration into a team sport. Create competitions around new strategies or gamify experiments to keep the energy high.
- Example: "Who can generate the most replies with a brand-new email subject line this week? The winner gets bragging rights—and coffee on me!"

When iteration feels like play, it's more likely to stick.

Iterate Like a Leader
Iteration isn't just about processes or tactics—it's about leadership. The more you model adaptability, curiosity, and a willingness to learn, the more your team will follow suit.
- Show them how you analyze your own performance.
- Share how you're experimenting with your leadership style.
- Celebrate their efforts to iterate—even when the results don't go as planned.

By embedding iteration into everything you do, you'll transform your team into a self-sustaining engine of growth and innovation.

In Summary: Trust Them, and They'll Deliver
Micromanagement is like watering a plant every five minutes—it doesn't help, and it stresses everyone out. Instead, focus on trust, accountability, and empowerment. When you give your BDRs the tools and freedom to succeed, consistency becomes second nature, and micromanagement becomes a thing of the past.

Chapter 5: Motivating Your BDR Team

Aligning Professional Goals with Personal Dreams

Every BDR has a reason they show up every day, and it's not just about hitting quotas. Sometimes it's about funding their dream trip, buying their first car, or supporting their family. Tapping into these personal motivators isn't just inspiring—it's a game-changer for performance. When managers connect professional goals to personal dreams, the work becomes more meaningful, and the results speak for themselves.

Real Stories, Real Impact

Here are examples of how personal dreams were tied directly to professional success:

- **From SDR to AE: The Family Responsibility**
  One of my SDRs was a former startup founder who needed to climb the ladder to an AE role. His goal wasn't just career growth—it was supporting his brother's education. Together, we aligned his personal need for financial stability with professional milestones that would accelerate his promotion. Every new deal he influenced wasn't just a win for the team—it was a step toward his family's future.

- **The Japan Trip Dream**
  Another SDR dreamed of traveling to Japan, but the catch was that she wanted to fund it entirely through her incentives. We created clear sales milestones tied to her variable pay. Every booked meeting wasn't just a metric—it was another sushi dinner or temple visit she was working toward. And yes, I am keeping my fingers crossed for her to make it happen.

- **The Bike Goal**
  One BDR had his eyes set on buying a bike. Instead of gifting it outright, we turned it into a goal linked to his variable pay. He crushed his targets, bought the bike, and learned the power of linking rewards to effort—a skill that fueled his professional growth.

- **A Car for Her Parents**
  For one BDR, her motivation was deeply personal: she wanted to surprise her parents with a car. By tying this dream to her performance goals, we helped her channel that drive into consistent pipeline contributions. The day she hit her milestone was a win for her family—and a moment of pride for the entire team.

- **The iPad Vision**
  Another BDR was determined to buy an iPad, but only with the money earned from hitting incentives. It wasn't about the iPad itself; it was about proving to herself that hard work pays off. Every booked meeting brought her closer to that goal, and the eventual purchase became a tangible symbol of her efforts.

Chapter 5: Motivating Your BDR Team

Why This Approach Works
- Goals Become Personal
  When work isn't just about metrics, it becomes meaningful. BDRs tie their efforts to something tangible, like a trip, a gift, or a major life goal.
- Motivation Goes Beyond the Paycheck
  Every outreach, every booked meeting, every follow-up is no longer "just a task"—it's a step closer to something they deeply care about.
- It Builds Trust and Loyalty
  When managers take the time to understand their team's dreams and actively work to connect those dreams to performance, it fosters a sense of loyalty. They feel seen and supported.

Connecting the Dots Between Goals and Dreams
Step 1: Understand What Drives Them
This isn't a surface-level, checkbox exercise—it's a genuine conversation. Find out what gets them excited and what they're working toward in their life beyond the office.
- **Questions to Ask:**
  - "If you could accomplish one personal goal this year, what would it be?"
  - "What's something you'd love to reward yourself with?"
  - "What motivates you to keep pushing through the tough days?"

Step 2: Make the Role a Stepping Stone
Once you know their dreams, show how their current role can help them get there.
- **For Aspiring AEs:**
  Highlight how developing BDR skills like lead qualification and objection handling lays the groundwork for AE success.
  - Example: "Your knack for turning cold leads into warm conversations is exactly what will make you a great AE."

- **For Future Entrepreneurs:**
  Connect their dream of running a business to the transferable skills they're mastering now.
  - Example: "Every cold call you make builds the confidence you'll need to pitch investors someday."
- **For Creative Dreamers:**
  Let them experiment with outreach strategies that align with their passions, like designing quirky LinkedIn posts or crafting storytelling emails.

Set Goals That Work for Both
It's not just about performance metrics—it's about dual-purpose goals that help BDRs grow while keeping them on track professionally.

Aligning Professional Goals with Personal Dreams

Chapter 5: Motivating Your BDR Team

- **Professional Goals:**
  - "Book 12 meetings this month, focusing on high-value accounts."
  - "Test a new social selling strategy and measure its response rates."
- **Dream-Aligned Goals:**
  - "Save enough incentive pay to fund your trip to Europe."
  - "Shadow an AE to learn negotiation skills for your next career step."

A Culture That Connects Goals and Dreams

Teams that thrive are built on more than quotas—they're built on shared purpose. Here's how you can make goal alignment part of your team's DNA:

- **Celebrate Personal Wins:**
  When someone hits a milestone—like buying their dream bike or booking a trip—make it a team celebration. Recognition builds camaraderie and inspires others to chase their own dreams.
- **Support Growth, Not Just Metrics:**
  Provide resources that align with their ambitions, whether it's mentorship, stretch assignments, or access to training that supports their long-term goals.
- **Revisit Goals Regularly:**
  Dreams evolve, and so should your approach. Use quarterly check-ins to revisit aspirations and adjust goals as needed.

Real Results, Real Lives

A BDR aiming for a marketing role was given the chance to lead email experimentation for her team. Her creative campaigns boosted response rates by 25%, and the skills she gained helped her land her dream job in the company's marketing department. Similarly, a BDR who wanted to fund his first international trip earned his bonus by hitting aggressive stretch goals, all while gaining the confidence to step into more senior roles.

Dream Big, Work Smart, Win Together

By aligning professional goals with personal dreams, you're creating a team that works not just harder but smarter. The result? BDRs who aren't just driven to hit numbers but are excited to grow, achieve, and thrive—both in and out of the office.

Chapter 5: Motivating Your BDR Team

Incentive Programs That Actually Work

BDRs are the engine of your sales team, and like any high-performance machine, they need the right fuel to stay motivated. But here's the catch: not all incentives work. Some fizzle out because they're too generic, while others fail because they're too complicated to understand. The best incentive programs inspire effort, reward creativity, and tie directly to what your team actually values.

What Makes a Great Incentive Program?
1. **It's Personal**
    - Great incentives speak to individual motivators. One BDR might love a shiny new gadget, while another is driven by public recognition. Generic rewards like "best performer gets a plaque" don't inspire anyone.
2. **It's Timely**
    - Long-term rewards are great, but short-term incentives keep momentum alive. Immediate gratification after hitting a milestone creates a direct link between effort and reward.
3. **It's Tied to Behavior, Not Just Results**
    - Rewarding only outcomes (like meetings booked) overlooks the critical behaviors (like quality outreach) that lead to those outcomes. Recognize the steps that build success.

Types of Incentives That Work

- **Financial Rewards with a Twist**
  Money talks, but it doesn't always have to shout. Creative spins on financial incentives add extra motivation.
    - Example: Instead of a generic cash bonus, offer a "choose your own adventure" incentive. BDRs can pick between options like concert tickets, spa days, or a paid subscription to their favorite service.
    - Real-Life Story: One company offered a "100% variable day" where BDRs who hit stretch goals could earn double their usual incentives for a single day of performance. The energy on the sales floor was electric.
- **Lifestyle Perks**
  Sometimes, it's not about the money. Offering perks that enhance life outside of work can drive just as much engagement.
    - Options like extra PTO, gym memberships, or wellness stipends show you value the person, not just the employee.
    - Example: A BDR team earned Friday afternoons off for hitting team-wide targets—a perk that boosted morale and performance.
- **Recognition-Based Rewards**
  For some BDRs, being acknowledged in front of their peers is more rewarding than anything monetary. Recognition builds confidence, camaraderie, and a sense of belonging.
    - **Ideas:**
- Create a "BDR of the Week" spotlight on Slack.

Chapter 5: Motivating Your BDR Team

- Offer a traveling trophy (or something quirky like a team mascot) for top performers.
  - Pro Move: Don't just recognize metrics. Celebrate creativity, teamwork, and problem-solving with equal enthusiasm.
- **Gamification**
Turning performance into a game adds energy and excitement. It's not just about winning—it's about creating a buzz around achievement.
  - Example: A "Pipeline Bingo" challenge where BDRs earn squares for booking certain types of meetings (e.g., "First-time buyer" or "Enterprise account"). Complete a row to win a prize.
- **Team-Based Incentives**
Incentive programs that encourage collaboration instead of competition foster stronger team dynamics.
  - Example: If the entire team exceeds the monthly target, everyone gets a shared reward like a team dinner or a paid outing.

How to Keep Incentive Programs Fresh
- **Rotate Rewards**
Don't let your incentives go stale. Rotate between cash bonuses, experience-based rewards, and professional growth opportunities to keep the team engaged.
- **Tie Rewards to Creativity**
Incentivize new ideas, like a competition for the most creative email subject line or the most engaging LinkedIn post.
- **Involve the Team in Choosing Rewards**
Ask your BDRs what would excite them most. When they're part of the process, buy-in skyrockets.

What to Avoid
- **Over-complication:**
If your team needs a manual to understand the rules, your incentive program is too complex. Keep it simple and intuitive.
- **One-Size-Fits-All Rewards:**
Incentives that don't resonate with individual preferences fail to motivate.
- **Only Recognizing Top Performers:**
Not everyone will be the top BDR, but effort, improvement, and teamwork deserve recognition too.

The Impact of Effective Incentives
An incentive program that works isn't just a feel-good initiative—it's a business accelerator. When your team feels motivated and valued, they push harder, think smarter, and bring their best to every call, email, and meeting.
Example: A SaaS company introduced a quarterly "Passion Project Bonus," where top performers received funding to pursue a personal passion. One BDR used it to enroll in a photography course, while another funded a weekend getaway with

Chapter 5: Motivating Your BDR Team

their family. Both came back more engaged and driven than ever.

Incentives That Inspire, Not Just Reward

At the end of the day, incentives are about more than prizes—they're about showing your team that their hard work matters. When you align rewards with what drives your BDRs, you're not just boosting performance—you're building a team that's excited to succeed.

Chapter 5: Motivating Your BDR Team

Recognizing and Celebrating Successes
Recognition isn't just a feel-good exercise—it's a strategic tool that fuels performance, builds morale, and fosters loyalty. When your team feels valued, they're more likely to bring their A-game. But the trick is making recognition authentic, timely, and impactful.

Why Recognition Matters
1. **It Reinforces Winning Behaviors:**
    - When BDRs see specific efforts recognized—like a creative email or extra persistence—it encourages them (and others) to replicate those behaviors.
2. **It Builds Confidence:**
    - Sales is tough. Recognition reminds your team that their hard work matters, even when they're facing rejection.
3. **It Fosters Loyalty:**
    - A simple "thank you" can be the difference between someone feeling like a cog in the machine or a valued team member.

Ways to Recognize Success
Public Shoutouts
Never underestimate the power of a well-placed compliment in front of peers. Public recognition boosts morale and gives others something to aspire to.
- **Team Meetings:** Start meetings by highlighting a standout performance or creative win.
    - Example: "Shoutout to Jess for booking a meeting with that tough-to-crack VP using a custom video pitch—brilliant work!"
- **Slack Channels:** Dedicate a channel for wins, big or small. It keeps the energy high and creates a record of achievements.

Celebrate the Journey, Not Just the Outcome
Sometimes, it's not about the win itself but the effort it took to get there.
- Creative Persistence: Acknowledge the BDR who finally landed a meeting after eight follow-ups.
    - Example: "Tom's persistence paid off! That enterprise lead who ghosted for three months? Meeting booked. Never give up, folks!"
- Process Wins: Celebrate improvements like higher response rates, better email open rates, or mastering a tough objection.

Team-wide Celebrations
Individual wins are great, but collective success builds camaraderie.
- **Milestone Rewards**: When the team hits a big target—like surpassing monthly pipeline goals—celebrate together. Whether it's a team lunch, happy hour, or an afternoon off, shared rewards strengthen bonds.
- **Gamified Recognition:** Create fun traditions, like a "BDR MVP" trophy that travels to the top performer each week, or quirky titles like "Follow-Up Ninja" or "Email Whisperer."

Chapter 5: Motivating Your BDR Team

Personalized Appreciation
One-size-fits-all recognition doesn't resonate. Tailor your approach to each BDR's personality and preferences.
- The Introvert's Win: Quiet achievers might prefer a thoughtful email or a handwritten note acknowledging their effort.
- The Spotlight Lover: For those who thrive on attention, make it big—public shoutouts, certificates, or even a quick feature in the company newsletter.

Celebrate Personal Milestones
Recognition doesn't always have to be about work. Celebrate life events like birthdays, anniversaries, or personal achievements.
- Example: When a BDR bought his first car with his incentives, the team surprised him with a car-themed cake.

What Recognition Looks Like in Action

Real-World Example 1:
A SaaS company implemented a "Wall of Wins" in their office (and digitally for remote teams). Every time a BDR booked a major meeting or solved a tricky challenge, their name and achievement went up for the whole company to see. It became a point of pride and motivation for the team.

Real-World Example 2:
Another team introduced a "Random Acts of Recognition" initiative. Managers would surprise BDRs with small rewards—like a coffee gift card or a shoutout in a leadership meeting—for unexpected wins. It reinforced the idea that every effort counts.

What to Avoid
1. **Generic Praise:**
   - Saying "Good job, team!" without specifics falls flat. Always highlight what made the effort special.
2. **Infrequent Recognition:**
   - Recognition works best when it's timely. Waiting until the end of the quarter to celebrate wins dilutes their impact.
3. **Overemphasis on Metrics:**
   - Celebrate creativity, effort, and teamwork alongside the numbers. Recognition should feel holistic.

The Ripple Effect of Recognition
When you celebrate your team's successes authentically and consistently, it doesn't just boost morale—it builds a culture of excellence. Recognized BDRs:
- Feel more confident in their abilities.
- Are more likely to share best practices with peers.
- Develop a deeper sense of belonging and loyalty to the team.

Chapter 5: Motivating Your BDR Team

President's Club and Chairman's Club: Celebrating Elite Performance
President's Club and Chairman's Club are the pinnacle of recognition for sales professionals. These exclusive rewards programs aren't just about trophies or vacations—they're about honoring the top contributors who consistently drive revenue, innovate, and inspire their peers.

What Are President's and Chairman's Clubs?
- **President's Club:** Typically designed to recognize the top 5–10% of sales performers within the company. It rewards consistent excellence in meeting or exceeding quotas.
- **Chairman's Club:** A step above President's Club, this honors the absolute best of the best—the elite performers whose impact transcends their numbers, often influencing team culture, strategy, and broader company success.

Both are about more than just performance; they're about celebrating leadership, creativity, and resilience.

Why They Matter
1. **Inspiration for the Team**
   - These programs create aspirational goals for BDRs and AEs alike. Knowing that hard work and innovation can lead to such recognition fuels motivation across the team.
2. **Reinforcement of Company Values**
   - Selection criteria often include not just revenue contribution but teamwork, creativity, and alignment with company culture.
3. **Loyalty and Retention**
   - Honoring top performers with prestigious rewards builds loyalty. They feel valued, recognized, and inspired to stay and continue their excellence.

The Emotional Payoff
For winners, these clubs represent the culmination of effort, creativity, and persistence. For the rest of the team, they're a beacon of what's possible. Done right, President's and Chairman's Clubs create a ripple effect of motivation, performance, and pride that resonates across the entire sales organization.

In Summary
Recognition is your secret weapon for building a high-performing, engaged, and loyal team. From public shoutouts to personalized moments, every gesture counts. Because when BDRs feel seen and valued, they don't just work harder—they work smarter, with passion and pride.

Chapter 5: Motivating Your BDR Team

Avoiding Burnout in a High-Pressure Role

BDRs are the lifeblood of the sales engine, but the role isn't for the faint of heart. Endless outreach, rejection, and the constant push to hit quotas can take a toll even on the most resilient team members. Burnout is the silent productivity killer, and tackling it isn't just about reducing stress—it's about fostering a sustainable, high-energy culture.

Understanding Burnout

Burnout doesn't happen overnight. It's a slow build, often starting with:
- Emotional exhaustion (feeling drained, even after a weekend).
- Cynicism (thinking, "What's the point?" after every no-show).
- Reduced performance (losing focus, forgetting to follow up).

Identifying these early signs is critical to creating interventions before they spiral.

Strategies to Prevent Burnout

1. Normalize Rest and Recovery

Sales culture often glamorizes "hustle" at the expense of well-being. Flip the script by making rest part of the strategy.
- Encourage PTO: Make sure BDRs take their vacation days—and truly unplug.
  - Pro Tip: Celebrate team members who return from a break recharged and ready to crush it.
- Build Buffer Days: Dedicate certain days to low-pressure activities like learning, brainstorming, or catching up on CRM hygiene.

2. Make Wins Visible (and Fun)

Burnout often comes from feeling like the hard work doesn't matter. Regularly celebrating wins, big or small, reminds BDRs of their impact.
- Create a "Wins of the Week" Ritual: Highlight successful calls, meetings booked, or even breakthroughs with tough prospects during team meetings.
- Gamify Progress: Introduce fun, low-stakes challenges like "First to Get a Call-Back Friday" with small prizes or bragging rights.

3. Focus on Development, Not Just Results

Constant pressure to deliver can feel suffocating without the balance of personal growth. Show BDRs that their role is a stepping stone, not a treadmill.
- Offer Skill-Building Opportunities: Let team members shadow AEs, take leadership courses, or explore other functions like marketing or operations.
- Set Growth Goals: Balance performance goals with development milestones, like mastering objection handling or increasing call efficiency.

4. Equip Managers to Spot the Signs

Burnout is easier to address when managers are trained to identify it early.
- Have Honest Check-Ins: Go beyond performance metrics in one-on-ones. Ask about stress levels, workload, and mental health in a way that feels supportive.

Chapter 5: Motivating Your BDR Team

  - Example: "How's your energy been lately? Anything I can help take off your plate?"
- Look for Behavioral Changes: Sudden dips in engagement, enthusiasm, or productivity are red flags that shouldn't be ignored.

Build Psychological Safety
In a high-pressure environment, BDRs need to feel they can speak up without fear of judgment.
- Encourage Openness: Normalize conversations about challenges, stress, and mental health.
- Model Vulnerability: Share your own experiences with stress or burnout and how you overcame them. This sets the tone for a culture of support.

Reframe Rejection
Rejection is inevitable, but it doesn't have to sting every time. Help your team reframe it as part of the process.
- Create a Culture of Resilience: Share stories about famous deals that started with 20 "no's" before a "yes."
- Celebrate Effort, Not Just Outcomes: Recognize BDRs for their creativity, persistence, or innovation, even if it doesn't immediately lead to a booked meeting.

Quick Wins for Burnout Prevention
1. Flexible Work Hours: Allow BDRs to work during their peak productivity times.
2. Mindfulness Breaks: Introduce short guided meditations or wellness apps to help reset during the day.
3. Buddy Systems: Pair BDRs to support each other during tough weeks.

Adding Some Fun: Friday Chill & Roast Sessions
Burnout isn't just about workload—it's about how stress is managed. One of the best ways to combat it? Laughter, camaraderie, and letting off steam. That's where the Friday Chill & Roast Session comes in.

This isn't your typical wrap-up meeting. It's a dedicated time for the team to unwind, reflect on the week, and poke a little fun at themselves (and each other) in a supportive, no-pressure environment.

What Happens During a Chill & Roast Session?
Celebrate the Wins (Humorously)
Kick things off by highlighting the week's biggest wins—but add a playful twist.
- Example: "Jess booked the meeting with the elusive VP of Marketing this week... after only sending 43 emails, 12 calls, and learning his dog's name. Persistence level: Jedi Master."

Avoiding Burnout in a High-Pressure Role

Chapter 5: Motivating Your BDR Team

Share the "Epic Fails"
Sometimes, the best way to let go of stress is to laugh at the moments that didn't go as planned.
- Example: "Shoutout to Alex, who confidently addressed a prospect as 'Karen' on a call... only to realize their name was clearly listed as 'Steve.' A true icon of improvisation!"

Peer Roasts (All in Good Fun)
BDRs take turns roasting each other's quirks or funny moments from the week—but the tone stays lighthearted and supportive.
- Example: "Shawn used the phrase 'circle back' in 14 consecutive emails this week. At this point, I think he's trying to build a NASCAR track."

Chill Out
End with something relaxing or fun:
- Play a quick trivia game (bonus points if it's sales-themed).
- Watch a funny sales video or meme collection together.
- Host a mock awards segment, like "Most Creative Follow-Up" or "Longest Email Ever Sent."

Why It Works
- Stress Release:
    - Humor is a natural stress reliever, helping the team decompress after a tough week.
- Fostering Connection:
    - These sessions build camaraderie, making the team feel more like a family and less like coworkers.
- Boosting Morale:
    - Ending the week with a laugh leaves everyone in a positive mood heading into the weekend.
- Reframing Challenges:
    - By laughing about mistakes, BDRs see them as learning experiences, not failures.

Real-World Example
At one of my teams, Friday Chill & Roast Sessions became the highlight of the week. BDRs who were initially hesitant ended up sharing their most cringe-worthy moments with pride, knowing it was a judgment-free zone. By the time the weekend rolled around, everyone felt lighter, more connected, and ready to tackle Monday with renewed energy.

Chapter 5: Motivating Your BDR Team

Team Book Reading, Mock Calls, and Call-Listening Sessions

Successful BDR teams aren't just built on activity metrics—they're built on continuous learning and collaboration. Activities like book discussions, mock calls, and call-listening sessions create an environment where BDRs sharpen their skills, share insights, and grow together. These aren't just "nice-to-haves"; they're powerful tools for building a culture of excellence.

1. Team Book Reading: Learning Together

A team that reads together, grows together. Book reading sessions go beyond skills—they expand perspectives and foster camaraderie.

How to Implement Team Book Reading

- Pick Relevant Reads: Choose books that inspire, educate, or challenge conventional thinking.
  - Examples:
    - "The Challenger Sale" for advanced selling techniques.
    - "Atomic Habits" for building productive routines.
    - "Never Split the Difference" for mastering negotiation.
- Create a Schedule: Divide the book into manageable sections and assign chapters for discussion during weekly or biweekly meetings.
- Facilitate Discussions: Make it interactive—ask team members how they'd apply the book's lessons to their day-to-day work.

The Benefits
- Sparks new ideas for outreach and objection handling.
- Builds team camaraderie through shared learning experiences.
- Reinforces the value of continuous self-improvement.

2. Mock Calls: Practicing in a Safe Space

Mock calls are the training ground for real conversations. They allow BDRs to practice without the pressure of a live prospect, building confidence and refining techniques.

How to Run Effective Mock Calls
- Assign Roles: Rotate roles so everyone gets to play both the BDR and the prospect. The latter role helps develop empathy and a deeper understanding of buyer objections.
- Use Real Scenarios: Base mock calls on actual challenges the team is facing—like re-engaging a dormant lead or overcoming a common objection.
- Record and Review: Record mock calls so participants can analyze tone, pacing, and phrasing. Feedback should be constructive, not critical.

The Benefits
- Prepares BDRs for tough conversations with confidence.
- Highlights areas for improvement, from tone to word choice.
- Encourages peer-to-peer learning and collaboration.

Chapter 5: Motivating Your BDR Team

3. Call-Listening Sessions: Learning from the Field
There's no better teacher than a real-world example. Listening to live or recorded calls gives BDRs a front-row seat to success (and sometimes failure).

How to Structure Call-Listening Sessions
- Choose Calls Strategically: Select a mix of successful calls and learning opportunities. The goal isn't to spotlight mistakes but to highlight lessons.
- Break Down Key Moments: Pause the recording at critical points—like how the opener was delivered or how an objection was handled—and discuss as a group.
- Encourage Open Dialogue: Let team members share their takeaways and suggestions for improvement.

The Benefits
- Reinforces best practices in a real-world context.
- Helps BDRs recognize patterns in successful conversations.
- Creates a safe space for constructive feedback and continuous improvement.

Why These Activities Matter
1. They Build Confidence: Mock calls and call-listening sessions provide the practice needed to turn theory into action.
2. They Foster Collaboration: Book discussions and team feedback sessions create a sense of shared ownership over success.
3. They Keep Learning Fresh: In a fast-paced role, these activities ensure skill-building isn't neglected.

Real-World Example
At a SaaS company, a monthly book club inspired a BDR to experiment with a negotiation technique from "Never Split the Difference." The result? A previously disengaged prospect re-engaged after the BDR reframed their ask during a follow-up call. Similarly, weekly call-listening sessions led to a 15% improvement in call-to-meeting conversions by identifying and fixing common objection-handling gaps.

The Bigger Picture
Activities like team book reading, mock calls, and call-listening sessions aren't just about developing individual skills—they're about building a culture of learning and collaboration. They transform a group of BDRs into a high-performing team, equipped with the tools, confidence, and camaraderie needed to excel.

Chapter 6: Career Planning for BDRs

Building a Career Path That Retains Talent

For many BDRs, their role is the first step in their professional journey—but if they don't see the next steps, they're likely to take their talent elsewhere. A well-designed career path isn't just a retention tool; it's a motivator, a loyalty builder, and a way to future-proof your team by developing homegrown talent.

When you invest in showing BDRs a clear and achievable path forward, they repay you with engagement, ambition, and results.

Why Career Pathing Matters

High-pressure roles like BDR demand more than quotas to keep people engaged. Without a vision for the future, talented reps burn out or leave for companies that promise better growth. Career pathing isn't just about promotions; it's about creating a system that keeps people inspired to bring their best every day.

- **Fuels Intrinsic Motivation**: BDRs want a guarantee that their hard work leads to something/somewhere meaningful.
- **Reduces Turnover**: High churn isn't just expensive, but it's demoralizing for the team. Career paths give reps a reason to stay.
- **Cultivates Leadership**: Promoting internally develops leaders who understand your culture, tools, and processes.
- **Attracts Top Performers**: Ambitious candidates are drawn to organizations that prioritize development.

How to Build an Effective Career Path
1. Map Out Clear Stages

Without a roadmap, career progression feels like a vague promise. Break the journey into actionable stages, each with defined goals and milestones.

Stage 1: Entry-Level BDR (0–12 Months)
- Focus: Mastering the fundamentals of prospecting, qualifying, and CRM usage.
- Milestones:
  - Consistently hit or exceed quota.
  - Deliver high-quality opportunities for AEs.
  - Show curiosity and eagerness to learn.

Stage 2: Senior BDR (12–24 Months)
- Focus: Becoming a trusted team leader and refining advanced skills like multi-threading accounts, handling objections, and mentoring peers.
- Milestones:
  - Develop creative strategies for engaging tough prospects.
  - Take on leadership responsibilities, such as training new hires.
  - Begin exploring potential next roles through stretch assignments or shadowing.

Chapter 6: Career Planning for BDRs

Stage 3: Specialized or Promoted Role (18–36 Months)
- Focus: Transitioning to a role that aligns with the BDR's strengths and career aspirations.
- Options:
    - Account Executive (AE): Manage the full sales cycle.
    - RevOps Specialist: Oversee CRM tools, analytics, and process optimization.
    - Marketing Strategist: Use prospecting insights to craft campaigns.
    - Team Lead: Manage and mentor a team of BDRs.

Stage 4: Strategic or Leadership Role (3+ Years)
- Focus: Taking on high-impact responsibilities that drive the organization forward.
- Examples:
    - BDR Manager or Director.
    - Enterprise AE managing high-value accounts.
    - Operations Manager optimizing cross-functional workflows.

2. Customize Career Paths to Individual Strengths

Every BDR brings unique talents to the table. Some thrive on the adrenaline of closing deals, while others are analytical problem-solvers or natural storytellers.

Career paths should reflect this diversity.
- **Assess Strengths Early**: Use one-on-one meetings and performance reviews to identify what excites and energizes each BDR.
- **Offer Flexible Tracks**: Let BDRs explore different areas through shadowing, projects, or temporary assignments.
    - Example: A data-savvy BDR might work with RevOps to refine lead-scoring models, while a creative BDR might collaborate with marketing on crafting outreach templates.

3. Invest in Skill Development

A career path isn't just a set of milestones—it's a journey of growth. Equip BDRs with the skills they need to succeed at every stage.
- Formal Training: Offer workshops on negotiation, social selling, or advanced CRM techniques.
- Stretch Assignments: Challenge BDRs with projects like leading a team brainstorming session or piloting a new prospecting strategy.
- Cross-Functional Exposure: Let BDRs shadow AEs, work with marketing, or collaborate on operational initiatives.

Example: A BDR who wanted to transition into marketing was tasked with creating an email campaign for a product launch. The campaign's success earned her a role in the marketing team.

Chapter 6: Career Planning for BDRs

4. Recognize and Celebrate Milestones
Progress doesn't always mean a promotion. Recognize incremental achievements to keep motivation high.
- **Skill Mastery**: Celebrate when a BDR improves their objection handling or boosts their response rates.
- **Team Contribution**s: Acknowledge reps who mentor peers, lead team projects, or innovate on outreach strategies.
- **Personal Growth**: Highlight moments where a BDR takes a bold step, like presenting in a team meeting or experimenting with a new approach.

5. Actively Support Transitions
The leap from BDR to AE—or any other role—can feel overwhelming. Managers should actively guide reps through this phase.
- **Mentorship Programs**: Pair transitioning reps with experienced colleagues in their desired role.
- **Structured Onboarding**: Create a roadmap for success in the new role, including expectations, metrics, and resources.

Example: A senior BDR preparing to become an AE was given six months to work alongside an AE on live deals, gradually taking on more responsibility until they were ready to handle their own accounts.

The Role of Managers in Career Pathing
Managers aren't just leaders—they're career architects.
- Have Meaningful Career Conversations: Ask questions that uncover aspirations:
  - "What excites you most about your future?"
  - "What skills would you love to build this year?"
- Be Their Advocate: Highlight your BDRs' achievements to leadership and advocate for stretch opportunities.
- Encourage Long-Term Thinking: Show how today's challenges prepare them for tomorrow's successes.

The Results of Career Pathing
1. Higher Retention Rates:
   - When BDRs see a future with your company, they stay longer.
2. Stronger Performance:
   - Motivated reps work harder, smarter, and more creatively.
3. A Leadership Pipeline:
   - Internally developed talent is better prepared to lead and innovate.

In Summary
A well-defined career path isn't just a benefit for your team—it's a strategic advantage for your business. By showing BDRs how their current role connects to their future ambitions, you create a culture where talent thrives, retention improves, and success compounds year after year.

Chapter 6: Career Planning for BDRs

Transitioning BDRs to AEs, RevOps, and Beyond

A role transition, whether to AE, RevOps, or marketing, is a leap that requires preparation. Without guidance, even your best BDRs can struggle to adapt. Preparing them isn't just about skill-building—it's about fostering confidence, setting expectations, and providing the right support to ensure they succeed in their next role.

1. Lay the Groundwork with Skills Development

Transitions often fail when skill gaps go unaddressed. Focus on building foundational skills that apply beyond the BDR role.

Key Areas to Develop

- Advanced Communication: Teach them how to lead deeper conversations, whether in negotiations or cross-functional collaboration.
  - Example: "How do you ask layered questions that reveal hidden pain points?"
- Time Management Mastery: Help them juggle competing priorities effectively. This is especially critical for roles like AE, where the sales cycle introduces new complexities.
- Data Fluency: Whether moving to RevOps or AE, understanding metrics like conversion rates, pipeline velocity, and forecast accuracy is invaluable.

Manager Tip

Create a "transition skills checklist" for each type of role. Use it during coaching sessions to track progress.

2. Provide Hands-On Experience

Learning by doing is one of the most effective ways to prepare BDRs for their next role.

Stretch Assignments

- For Aspiring AEs: Assign mini-deal cycles where they handle discovery and early negotiations before handing off to a mentor.
- For RevOps Candidates: Have them lead a CRM cleanup project or analyze team performance metrics.
- For Marketing Explorers: Involve them in creating messaging for campaigns or social selling initiatives.

Shadowing Opportunities

- Pair BDRs with team members in their target role for 2–4 weeks to observe processes, workflows, and challenges firsthand.

3. Create a Transition Timeline

A clear timeline ensures the process feels structured and achievable.

Phased Approach

- Exploration (0–3 Months): The BDR starts shadowing and taking on small projects in their target area.
- Active Preparation (3–6 Months): They handle stretch assignments

Chapter 6: Career Planning for BDRs

- independently with periodic coaching.
- Role Transition (6+ Months): With skills and experience in place, they fully step into the new role.

Manager Tip
Align the timeline with quarterly goals and performance reviews to integrate the process into existing workflows.

4. Focus on Confidence and Mindset
Transitioning roles is as much about mindset as it is about skills. Help BDRs overcome self-doubt and embrace the challenge.
Normalize Mistakes
- Reassure them that missteps are part of growth. Share examples of successful transitions that included learning curves.

Highlight Transferable Skills
- Show them how their BDR experience sets them up for success.
  - Example: "Your persistence and creativity in outreach will help you as an AE when navigating complex deal cycles."

Celebrate Progress
- Recognize their milestones during the transition process—whether it's running their first solo negotiation or successfully completing a data analysis project.

5. Build a Strong Support System
Transitions are easier with guidance. Create a network of mentors and resources for transitioning BDRs.
Mentorship Programs
- Pair transitioning BDRs with experienced professionals in their target role for guidance and advice.

Onboarding Buddy System
- Assign a peer mentor during their first 90 days in the new role to help navigate challenges.

Manager's Role
- Stay actively involved in their transition, providing regular feedback and encouragement.

6. Manage Expectations
The excitement of a new role can sometimes lead to unrealistic expectations. Ground the transition in reality.
Set Clear Success Metrics
- Define what "good" looks like in the new role, including measurable milestones for the first 90 days.

Communicate Challenges
- Be upfront about the difficulties they may face, but frame them as opportunities to grow.

Transitioning BDRs to AEs, RevOps, and Beyond

Chapter 6: Career Planning for BDRs

- Example: "As an AE, you'll need to manage your own pipeline, which can be challenging at first. But your organizational skills as a BDR have already prepared you for this."

The Payoff

When BDRs are prepared for their next role, they hit the ground running instead of struggling to adapt. This investment in preparation:
- Boosts their confidence and performance.
- Reduces ramp time in their new role.
- Strengthens loyalty to your organization, as they see you're committed to their growth.

Chapter 6: Career Planning for BDRs

Tailoring Development Plans to Individual Strengths
No two BDRs are the same, and a one-size-fits-all approach to development rarely works. By tailoring growth plans to each individual's unique strengths, you empower your team to excel in their roles and prepare for the next step in their careers. This approach not only drives performance but also fosters loyalty and engagement.

Why Focus on Individual Strengths?
- Faster Skill Mastery: BDRs progress more quickly when building on their natural abilities.
- Higher Engagement: Personalization makes development plans feel relevant and achievable.
- Stronger Team Performance: Leveraging diverse strengths creates a well-rounded, high-performing team.

Steps to Tailor Development Plans
1. Identify Strengths Early
The first step is understanding what each BDR naturally excels at.
- Observation: Watch for patterns in their performance.
    - Example: "Does this BDR consistently book meetings with creative email campaigns or excel at objection handling?"
- Data-Driven Insights: Use metrics like email open rates, call conversion rates, or response times to uncover areas of excellence.
- Ask Them: During 1:1s, discuss what they enjoy most and feel most confident doing.

2. Align Strengths with Career Aspirations
Once you've identified their strengths, connect them to their future goals.
- Creative Thinkers: If they excel at crafting personalized emails, suggest a potential future in marketing or content strategy.
- Data-Driven Performers: If they thrive on metrics, guide them toward roles in RevOps or analytics.
- Relationship Builders: Those who naturally connect with prospects may be suited for AE or customer success roles.

3. Set Development Goals Around Strengths
Design goals that amplify their strengths while addressing key skill gaps.
- Example Goals:
    - For a creative thinker: "Experiment with 3 new outreach strategies this month and share results with the team."
    - For a data-driven performer: "Analyze response trends from 50 recent prospects to refine outreach timing."

Chapter 6: Career Planning for BDRs

4. Provide Targeted Learning Opportunities
Not all training programs are created equal. Focus on those that cater to individual strengths.
- Creative BDRs: Offer courses on storytelling or design thinking.
- Analytical BDRs: Provide tools and training on CRM reporting or lead scoring.
- Relationship-Oriented BDRs: Introduce negotiation workshops or mock client presentations.

5. Encourage Stretch Assignments
Push BDRs slightly outside their comfort zones to help them grow while still leveraging their strengths.
- Example: A BDR skilled in objection handling could lead a team training session on overcoming the toughest prospect pushbacks.

The Role of Managers
1. Be a Strengths Detective: Regularly assess and adapt development plans as your BDRs grow.
2. Offer Continuous Feedback: Highlight how their strengths are impacting team and individual success.
3. Create a Feedback Loop: Involve BDRs in refining their own development plans.

Real-World Example
At a tech company, one BDR with a knack for relationship-building was given a stretch goal to lead an account reactivation campaign. Her ability to re-engage dormant leads increased team pipeline contribution by 20%, and she gained the confidence to pursue an Account Manager role.

The Payoff
Tailored development plans build confidence, accelerate growth, and create a culture where every BDR feels valued for their unique contributions. By investing in their strengths today, you're preparing them for success tomorrow.

Chapter 6: Career Planning for BDRs

The Role of Mentorship and Coaching: Building a Stronger BDR Team

When it comes to leading a BDR team, mentorship and coaching aren't just buzzwords—they're the lifeblood of sustainable success. While metrics and playbooks provide the structure, it's mentorship and coaching that breathe life into the process, transforming potential into performance.

Why Mentorship and Coaching Matter

Think of your BDR team as a garden. Metrics are the sunlight, processes are the soil, but mentorship and coaching are the water—constant, essential, and tailored to the needs of each plant. Without them, even the best frameworks will struggle to yield results.

- Mentorship provides the big picture, offering guidance on career growth, personal development, and navigating challenges beyond the day-to-day grind.
- Coaching is about sharpening execution, focusing on the finer points of performance—like refining outreach techniques, handling objections, or mastering tools.

Together, they don't just create better performers; they build confident, future-ready professionals who can thrive in any role.

How Mentorship Transforms Team Culture

Mentorship isn't a perk—it's a strategic necessity for retaining talent and fostering engagement. Here's how it changes the game:

- **Empowerment Through Guidance:**
  When BDRs know someone is invested in their success, they're more likely to push through challenges and stay motivated. A good mentor offers perspective: "That tough quarter? It's a stepping stone, not a roadblock."
- **Building Career Pathways:**
  Talented BDRs often leave when they feel stuck. Mentors help them see the bigger picture—how today's hustle builds tomorrow's opportunities.
- **Fostering Trust and Retention:**
  Mentorship creates an environment where team members feel valued. When they know their leaders care about their growth, they're more likely to stick around.

Coaching: The Heart of Skill Development

Coaching is where leaders transition from managing tasks to developing people. It's the day-to-day work of helping BDRs close skill gaps, grow in confidence, and reach new heights.

Here's how to make coaching work for your team:
- **Tailor Sessions to Individual Needs:**
  - No two BDRs are the same. One might struggle with objection handling, while another needs help crafting better emails. Customize your coaching

Chapter 6: Career Planning for BDRs

to address these unique challenges.
- Example: Use call recordings to identify patterns in objection handling, then workshop better responses.

- **Coach in the Moment:**
    - Great coaching isn't reserved for one-on-ones. Whether it's giving feedback after a call or troubleshooting during a pipeline review, seize opportunities to teach in real time.

- **Use Data to Guide Discussions:**
    - Dashboards and KPIs aren't just for management—they're tools for coaching. Help BDRs interpret their own performance metrics to identify strengths and areas for improvement.

- **Make Role-Playing a Habit:**
    - Practice makes perfect, and role-playing is the ultimate practice ground. Regular mock calls, objection drills, and email reviews can turn weak points into strong suits.

Balancing Mentorship and Coaching
The best leaders wear both hats seamlessly. Here's how to strike the right balance:
- Mentor when discussing the future:
    - Career paths, long-term goals, and personal development.
    - Example: A monthly check-in focused on how a BDR's strengths align with a future AE role.
- Coach when improving execution:
    - Day-to-day tasks, immediate goals, and refining techniques.
    - Example: A post-call review to pinpoint where an opportunity was lost and how to recover next time.

Mentorship in Action: Setting the Example
- Create Peer-Mentorship Programs:
    - Pair senior BDRs with new hires to foster a collaborative environment. A seasoned BDR can provide real-world insights that supplement formal training.
    - Example: The "Buddy System"—where every new hire shadows an experienced rep for their first 30 days.
- Be the Mentor You Wish You Had:
    - Share your own career journey, lessons learned, and moments of failure. This vulnerability creates a connection and builds trust.

Coaching as a Continuous Loop
Coaching isn't a one-and-done task—it's an ongoing loop:
- Observe: Watch calls, review emails, and analyze metrics to understand performance.

Chapter 6: Career Planning for BDRs

- Feedback: Deliver clear, actionable insights in a way that motivates rather than deflates.
- Practice: Role-play, refine techniques, and encourage experimentation.
- Repeat: Revisit progress and adjust strategies as needed.

Real Talk: What Makes a Great Mentor or Coach
Let's not sugarcoat it: being a mentor or coach requires effort, patience, and humility. The best leaders:
- Listen First: Coaching isn't about talking—it's about understanding. Ask questions before offering advice.
- Celebrate Wins, Big and Small: Recognition builds momentum. Don't just celebrate booked meetings; celebrate breakthroughs in skills or mindset.
- Know When to Step Back: True mentorship means empowering your team to find their own solutions.

The Long-Term Impact of Mentorship and Coaching
BDRs who feel supported are:
- More Engaged: They're invested in the team's success because they feel the team is invested in theirs.
- More Resilient: Mentorship and coaching provide the tools to handle rejection and navigate challenges with confidence.
- More Likely to Stay: When BDRs see a clear path forward, they'll stick around to walk it.

Closing Thought:
Mentorship and coaching aren't just tasks on your to-do list—they're the most important work you'll do as a leader. The tools and processes you implement might build a pipeline, but the trust and confidence you instill in your team will build the future. Be the leader who inspires, not just the one who manages.

Chapter 7: Transition Planning

Promoting from Within: The Do's and Don'ts

Promotions are pivotal moments in a BDR team's lifecycle. Handled well, they inspire the entire team, demonstrate career growth opportunities, and retain top talent. Done poorly, they can lead to resentment, confusion, and even turnover. To navigate this minefield, you need a clear strategy rooted in fairness, transparency, and preparation.

The Do's of Promoting from Within

- **Start with Clear Criteria:**
  - Promotions shouldn't feel like a surprise or a mystery. From Day 1, your BDRs should understand what's required to advance. Tie promotions to measurable performance, demonstrated leadership, and readiness for new challenges.
  - Example: Create a "Career Progression Scorecard" that outlines key metrics (e.g., quota attainment, peer mentorship), skills (e.g., advanced objection handling, multi-threading accounts), and behaviors (e.g., collaboration, initiative).
- **Develop Future Leaders Early:**
  - Leadership skills don't magically appear with a new title. Identify potential leaders early and give them opportunities to grow through stretch assignments or informal mentorship roles.
  - Example: Assign high-performing BDRs to train new hires, lead call-listening sessions, or refine team processes.
- **Celebrate the Win:**
  - Promotions are as much about the individual as they are about the team. Announce promotions in a way that highlights both the BDR's achievements and how their growth benefits the team.
  - Example: "Jess has consistently gone above and beyond, not only hitting her numbers but mentoring new hires. Her promotion to AE shows what's possible for all of us."
- **Provide the Right Support:**
  - Moving into a new role can be intimidating, even for top performers. Equip them with the tools, training, and coaching they need to succeed.
  - Example: A new AE should receive onboarding tailored to selling, even if they've mastered prospecting.

The Don'ts of Promoting from Within

- **Don't Promote Based Solely on Performance:**
  - The best BDR doesn't automatically make the best AE or team lead. Leadership and new role readiness require different skill sets.
  - Example: If a BDR excels at booking meetings but struggles with collaboration or handling objections, they may not yet be ready to lead or sell.

Chapter 7: Transition Planning

- Don't Neglect the Team Dynamic:
  - A promotion changes team dynamics. Be mindful of how the team perceives it, especially if others were in the running.
  - Solution: Be transparent about why the decision was made and reiterate how the process is designed to reward everyone's growth.
- Don't Rush the Decision:
  - Premature promotions set employees up to fail. Ensure readiness through thorough assessments and role-specific training.
- Don't Forget Succession Planning:
  - When you promote a top performer, you create a gap in the BDR team. Have a plan in place to backfill their workload seamlessly.
  - Example: Train multiple high performers to step into leadership or expanded responsibilities if needed.

Tying It Back to Mentorship and Coaching
As discussed in the previous chapter, mentorship plays a critical role in preparing BDRs for promotions. Regular coaching sessions help identify strengths and areas for growth, ensuring that when the time comes, the right person is ready to step up.

The Impact on Team Morale: When Promotions Go Right (or Wrong)
When handled well, promotions are a powerful motivator. They signal to the team that hard work, growth, and contributions are recognized and rewarded. This boosts morale, fosters healthy competition, and reinforces a culture of ambition and excellence. On the flip side, mishandled promotions can be demoralizing. If the process feels opaque, unfair, or politically driven, it breeds resentment, disengagement, and even attrition. Team members may feel their efforts are undervalued, leading to a toxic environment where people stop striving for growth. As a leader, how you manage promotions sends a clear message about what your team values—make sure it's the right one.

Closing Thought
Promotions are a testament to your team's success and your ability as a leader to nurture talent. When done thoughtfully, they don't just elevate one person—they inspire the entire team to strive for growth. Keep your process fair, transparent, and tied to the bigger picture of your team's development.

Chapter 7: Transition Planning

Succession Planning for Critical Roles

Every high-performing BDR team has key players whose absence could disrupt workflows, morale, and results. Whether it's a team lead, a top-performing BDR, or even you as the leader, a sudden departure can leave a gap that's difficult to fill. Succession planning is your safety net, ensuring continuity and stability no matter what challenges arise.

Why Succession Planning Matters

Succession planning isn't just about preparing for the worst—it's about proactively building a resilient, adaptable team. Here's why it's critical:

1. Mitigating Risk: Unexpected departures can derail momentum. Succession planning ensures that knowledge, processes, and performance don't suffer.
2. Fostering Growth: Identifying potential successors creates opportunities for team members to develop leadership and advanced skills.
3. Building a Culture of Preparedness: Teams with succession plans are more agile, better equipped to handle change, and less dependent on any single individual.

Steps to Effective Succession Planning

- **Identify Critical Roles**
  Not every position requires a succession plan. Focus on roles that are central to your team's success:
  - Team Leads or Senior BDRs: They often hold institutional knowledge and set the tone for the team.
  - Specialized BDRs: If someone excels at handling a particular vertical or market segment, their absence could create a bottleneck.
  - Your Role as Leader: A well-functioning team should be able to maintain momentum even if you're out of the picture temporarily.

- **Assess and Develop Potential Successors**
  Succession isn't about replacing someone—it's about preparing others to step into larger roles when the time comes. Start by identifying team members with leadership potential:
  - Use Performance and Potential as Guides: Look for individuals who not only excel at their current roles but also show adaptability, initiative, and the ability to influence others.
  - Focus on Skills Development: Provide stretch assignments to build readiness.
    - Example: Assign a high-performing BDR to lead a weekly stand-up or manage a small project like refining outreach cadences.
  - Leverage Mentorship and Coaching: Create growth plans tailored to individual strengths and career goals.
    - Reference: Tie this back to Chapter 6's mentorship strategies for practical implementation.

Chapter 7: Transition Planning

- Document Processes and Knowledge
  Institutional knowledge shouldn't live in one person's head. If critical team members leave, their expertise shouldn't leave with them.
  - Create Playbooks: Ensure workflows, scripts, and key processes are documented and easily accessible.
    - Example: Build a shared repository for email templates, call scripts, and prospecting strategies.
  - Shadowing Programs: Allow potential successors to shadow experienced team members to absorb hands-on knowledge.

- **Communicate the Plan**
  Transparency is key. Succession planning shouldn't feel like a secretive process—it's a strategy for growth.
  - Set Expectations: Let your team know that development opportunities align with the organization's needs.
  - Balance Transparency: While it's good to share that someone is being groomed for growth, avoid prematurely labeling someone as a successor, which could create tension or complacency.

- **Test and Refine**
  A succession plan is only as good as its execution. Regularly test your plan to ensure it's realistic:
  - Simulate Scenarios:
    - Example: Have a senior BDR step into your role for a week while you focus on higher-level strategic tasks. Use this as an opportunity to assess their readiness and provide feedback.
  - Gather Feedback: Involve your team in refining the process. What worked? What felt unclear?

When It's Done Right
A solid succession plan doesn't just safeguard against disruptions—it energizes your team. It shows that you're invested in their growth and see potential in their contributions. This builds trust, inspires engagement, and creates a culture of readiness. Team members are more likely to stay when they see a clear path for their development.

When It's Done Wrong
Failure to plan creates vulnerability. If a critical role suddenly becomes vacant, the scramble to fill the gap can lead to poor decision-making, resentment among remaining team members, and a decline in performance. Worse, a lack of planning signals to the team that their future isn't a priority—an attitude that can accelerate turnover.

Chapter 7: Transition Planning

Proactive Leadership: Building a Resilient Team – Cheatsheet
Building resilience in your BDR team ensures stability and success, even in the face of change. Here's how to make it happen:

1. Foster Shared Ownership
- Encourage team collaboration through knowledge sharing and "skills swap" sessions.
- Celebrate team wins to reinforce a collective mindset over individual competition.

2. Build Role Redundancy
- Cross-train team members on critical tasks to avoid bottlenecks.
- Rotate leadership roles to prepare multiple successors for key positions.

3. Prioritize Talent Development
- Regularly discuss career aspirations and create tailored growth plans.
- Assign stretch projects to build new skills and confidence.
- Use continuous feedback to challenge and support individual development.

4. Strengthen Processes and Systems
- Document playbooks for key tasks and roles, updating them quarterly.
- Automate repetitive tasks with tools to reduce dependency on individuals.

5. Promote Trust and Autonomy
- Empower BDRs to make decisions and support them, even if mistakes happen.
- Be transparent about succession planning to align team goals with individual growth.

6. Prepare for Your Own Transition
- Develop a second-in-command to handle operations when you're unavailable.
- Document your leadership methods (e.g., feedback processes, goal-setting) as a playbook for continuity.

Key Takeaway: A resilient team thrives on shared knowledge, adaptable leadership, and strong systems. Great leaders focus on creating independence, not dependence.

Chapter 7: Transition Planning

Managing Knowledge Transfer Effectively: A Phased Approach with Checklists

Effective knowledge transfer ensures continuity, reduces onboarding time, and keeps the team running smoothly when key players move on. Here's a phased approach to systematize knowledge sharing.

Phase 1: Prepare
Goal: Identify critical knowledge and create a plan for sharing it.
Checklist:
- Identify key roles and the specific knowledge tied to them (e.g., scripts, outreach strategies, workflows).
- Determine tools for documentation and sharing (e.g., Google Drive, Notion, CRM knowledge base).
- Assign ownership of knowledge transfer for each critical area (e.g., senior BDR for prospecting best practices).

Phase 2: Document
Goal: Create accessible, organized resources for team use.
Checklist:
- Develop playbooks for essential processes:
    - Prospecting cadences.
    - Objection-handling scripts.
    - CRM workflows and tips.
- Use templates to ensure consistency across documentation.
- Record training sessions, team meetings, and call reviews for on-demand access.
- Store all resources in a centralized, easily accessible location.

Phase 3: Share
Goal: Encourage team collaboration and regular knowledge exchange.
Checklist:
- Schedule monthly knowledge-sharing sessions.
    - Example: "What's working" presentations from top-performing BDRs.
- Implement a buddy system:
    - Pair new hires with experienced team members for hands-on training.
- Assign peer-led training on specific tools or processes (e.g., using LinkedIn Sales Navigator effectively).
- Celebrate team members who contribute valuable insights to the knowledge base.

Phase 4: Cross-Train
Goal: Build redundancy to reduce reliance on any single individual.
Checklist:
- Identify specialized skills (e.g., enterprise lead handling) and train at least two other team members on those tasks.

Chapter 7: Transition Planning

- Rotate responsibilities temporarily to allow team members to practice new roles.
- Schedule shadowing sessions for junior BDRs to observe senior colleagues' workflows.

Phase 5: Transition
Goal: Ensure seamless handovers during departures or role changes.
Checklist:
- Conduct exit interviews to gather undocumented insights from departing employees.
- Create a transition document for each departing role, covering:
    - Key tasks and responsibilities.
    - In-progress projects.
    - Contact information for important stakeholders.
- Schedule overlap time between the departing employee and their replacement, if possible.

Phase 6: Evaluate and Improve
Goal: Continuously refine the knowledge transfer process.
Checklist:
- Gather feedback from team members on the usefulness of documentation and training sessions.
- Update playbooks and knowledge bases quarterly to reflect changes in processes or strategies.
- Identify gaps in current knowledge transfer practices and implement solutions.

Key Takeaway: Build a Culture of Knowledge Sharing
Knowledge transfer isn't a single event; it's a habit embedded in your team's culture. A phased approach ensures your team remains adaptable and resilient, no matter who stays, goes, or joins.

Chapter 7: Transition Planning

Resilience in Action: What to Do When the Unexpected Happens
Change is inevitable in any team. Whether it's a sudden departure, a shift in strategy, or an external challenge like market fluctuations, the dynamics of your BDR team will inevitably be tested. These moments reveal the strength of your leadership and the resilience of your team. How you navigate these changes sets the tone for the future—not just in overcoming the immediate issue, but in building a team that thrives through uncertainty.

Change and Its Ripple Effect on the Team
When the unexpected happens, the impact on your team goes beyond the immediate logistical challenges. Changes—like losing a senior BDR or adapting to a new company directive—can disrupt morale, workloads, and even team cohesion. But handled well, these moments can also become opportunities to grow stronger together.

- **Morale and Stability:**
  Sudden changes can create anxiety, especially if the team feels unprepared. They might question their own roles or wonder if more changes are on the horizon.
  - Leadership's Role: This is your chance to step up as a stabilizing force. Acknowledge the uncertainty, but reinforce your team's value and the systems in place to ensure continued success.
- **Redistribution of Workloads:**
  Change often means someone has to pick up the slack. Whether it's reallocating accounts or shifting outreach strategies, the team must adjust to new demands.
  - Opportunity for Growth: Reassign responsibilities in a way that aligns with team members' aspirations. For example, let a junior BDR take on a high-profile account to prove their capabilities.
- **Team Dynamics:**
  Changes—especially departures—can alter team chemistry. A strong leader recognizes the need to rebuild or even redefine team dynamics.
  - Strengthening Bonds: Use this as a chance to unite the team. Encourage open communication and foster a shared sense of purpose.

Adapting to the Unexpected
Change is inevitable, but disruption doesn't have to be. Resilient teams adapt quickly and emerge stronger. Here's how to guide your team through change effectively:

- **Reaffirm Core Values and Goals:**
  When everything feels uncertain, grounding your team in what remains constant helps maintain focus.
  - Example: If a senior BDR leaves, remind the team: "Our mission hasn't changed—we're here to connect with prospects and drive value. Each of you plays a critical role in that."

Chapter 7: Transition Planning

- **Leverage Systems to Minimize Disruption:**
  Strong systems can carry your team through turbulent times. Playbooks, shared repositories, and clear processes ensure continuity even when roles shift.
  - Example: If a key player departs, a well-documented playbook can ensure their strategies and workflows remain accessible to the team.
- **Encourage Flexibility:**
  Resilient teams are adaptable. Encourage your team to view change as a chance to grow, learn, and test new approaches.
  - Example: If quotas suddenly increase, challenge your team to experiment with outreach tactics that drive faster results, like video prospecting or multi-threading accounts.

Leadership in Times of Change

Leadership isn't tested during smooth sailing; it's tested when the waters get rough. How you handle change directly impacts your team's ability to rebound and thrive.

- **Be Transparent:**
  Your team doesn't need every detail, but they need honesty. Openly address the change, explain its impact, and outline your plan to move forward.
  - Example Statement: "Losing [Name] is a big shift for us, but it's also a chance for others to step up. Here's how we're redistributing responsibilities while we plan for a long-term solution."
- **Focus on Individual and Team Growth:**
  Change creates opportunities for development. Frame transitions as chances for the team to learn new skills or take on bigger responsibilities.
  - Example: If a leadership role opens, encourage high-potential BDRs to shadow you or co-lead initiatives.
- **Rebuild Confidence:**
  After the initial shock of change, your team needs to feel empowered to succeed. Celebrate small wins, recognize contributions, and remind them of their strengths.
  - Example: "I know this week has been tough, but the way you've rallied together has been incredible. It shows just how capable this team is."

Turning Challenges into Opportunities

Resilience isn't just about enduring change—it's about leveraging it for growth. When handled with intention, unexpected shifts can strengthen your team's adaptability, collaboration, and confidence.

- **Growth Through Change**: Transitions often reveal hidden strengths within your team. A junior BDR taking on new responsibilities may surprise you with their capability and initiative.

Chapter 7: Transition Planning

- **Evolving Team Identity**: Each change gives your team a chance to redefine how they work together. Use this moment to foster a culture of adaptability and shared accountability.
- **Improved Systems**: Challenges often expose gaps in your processes. Addressing them now builds a more efficient, scalable team for the future.

Cheat Sheet: Transition Planning and Building Resilient Teams

When planning for transitions, resilience is the secret weapon that keeps your team thriving instead of just surviving. Use this cheat sheet to navigate change with purpose, clarity, and impact.

1. Preparing for Transitions

- Create a Playbook: Document processes for onboarding, role shifts, and exits to minimize disruption.
- Identify Key Roles: Map out critical positions and the skills required to fill them.
- Train Future Leaders: Start mentoring potential successors before transitions are even on the horizon.

Quick Tip: Think of transition planning like fire drills—prepare before there's smoke.

2. Leading During Change

- Be Transparent: Share the "why" behind transitions with your team to build trust and reduce anxiety.
- Celebrate Adaptability: Recognize individuals and teams who embrace change with grace.
- Stay Calm: Your energy sets the tone—stay steady and focused to keep morale high.

Pro Tip: "I don't know yet, but I'll find out" is a perfectly acceptable answer.

3. Building Resilience

- Encourage Continuous Feedback: Use weekly pulse checks to understand what's working and what's not.
  - Example: "What's one thing slowing you down this week, and how can we fix it?"
- Train for Change: Run "what-if" scenarios to help your team practice adaptability.
  - Example: "What would we do if a major client churned tomorrow?"
- Celebrate Small Wins: Use quick successes to rebuild confidence after disruptions.

Key Reminder: Resilience isn't about avoiding challenges—it's about bouncing back stronger.

4. Managing Departures

- Handle Exits Gracefully: Celebrate departing team members' contributions and ensure smooth handoffs.
- Prioritize Knowledge Transfer: Document workflows and key insights before

Chapter 7: Transition Planning

team members leave.
- Focus on Continuity: Communicate clear interim plans to avoid confusion and maintain momentum.

Bonus Tip: Treat departures as an opportunity to evaluate and improve team dynamics.

5. Redefining Success Post-Transition
- Reassess Metrics: Adjust KPIs to align with new roles, team structures, or goals.
- Rebuild Team Identity: Use change as an opportunity to strengthen collaboration and culture.
- Focus on Long-Term Wins: Keep your team focused on the bigger picture while addressing short-term challenges.

Closing Thought
Resilient teams don't fear change—they embrace it as an opportunity to grow stronger and more connected. As a leader, your ability to guide the team through the unexpected doesn't just solve the problem at hand; it sets the stage for future success. Change is inevitable, but disruption is optional—when you lead with purpose, your team will rise to the challenge.

Chapter 8: Frameworks and Processes

Developing a Scalable Playbook: The No-Nonsense Guide

Think of your playbook as the DNA of your BDR team. It's the operating manual that turns chaos into consistency. Done right, it's a living, breathing resource that grows alongside your team. Done wrong, it's a dusty PDF no one opens. Let's create the version your team will actually use.

Step 1: Start with What You Have

Forget perfection. The best playbooks start by documenting what already works. Don't overthink it—just get it on paper.

- Sit with your top-performing BDRs: Ask them to walk you through how they prep, prospect, and close meetings. What tools do they swear by? What do they avoid?
- Find the hidden gems: Look for email templates that get replies, call openings that break the ice, and cadences that work across industries.

Action: Spend a week shadowing your team and jotting down what works. Boom—you've got the skeleton of your playbook.

Step 2: Validate It with Data

Good playbooks aren't built on hunches; they're built on evidence. Take a hard look at what's driving success.

- Wins and Losses:
   - What's common across deals that close?
   - Why did deals fall apart? Missed timing? Bad fit? Poor messaging? Write it down.
- PMF Reality Check:
   - Ask your customers why they bought. What problem did you solve for them?
   - Interview lost leads. (Yes, it's awkward—but it's gold.)

Action: Create two columns: "Why We Win" and "Why We Lose." Then build your cadences and objection-handling around that.

Step 3: Build the Persona Bible

Prospects aren't all the same, and neither are your pitches. Create a cheat sheet for the team:

- Persona Snapshot: Titles, roles, and industries you target.
   - Example: "Director of IT at a 100–500 employee SaaS company."
- Pain Points: What keeps them up at night?
   - Example: "Scaling infrastructure without blowing the budget."
- Hooks: Why they'd care about what you're selling.
   - Example: "We cut scaling costs by 30% for companies like XYZ."

Pro Tip: Keep it short and actionable. If it doesn't fit on one page, it's too much.

Chapter 8: Frameworks and Processes

Step 4: Make It a Living Playbook
Your playbook is useless if it's outdated by the time a new hire joins. Treat it like a Google Doc, not a stone tablet.
- Monthly Updates: Dedicate 15 minutes in team meetings to share "what's working now."
- Feedback Loops: Ask the team: "What's missing? What's outdated?"
- Include Experiments: Tried a crazy new LinkedIn message that worked? Add it to the playbook.

Real Talk: The second you stop updating your playbook, your team stops using it. Make it evolve with them.

Step 5: Know Thy Competition
Don't just prepare your team to sell your product; prepare them to beat competitors.
- Spy Smartly: Sign up for competitors' newsletters, download their white papers, and attend their webinars.
- Debrief Prospects: If someone chooses a competitor, ask them why. What did they love? What were the trade-offs?
- Build Comparison Sheets: Outline where you win and where they might have an edge. Teach your team how to position around it.

Example: "Competitor X has lower pricing, but we're ROI-positive in 3 months because of XYZ feature. Here's how to show them the math."

Step 6: Make It Stupid Simple
If your playbook feels like a corporate manual, no one will read it. Make it user-friendly.
- Bite-Sized Sections: Instead of a 50-page doc, think of your playbook as a collection of cheat sheets.
- Visuals Over Text: Use screenshots, flowcharts, and video walkthroughs.
- Searchable and Accessible: Store it in Notion, Confluence, or a CRM add-on—wherever your team already works.

Step 7: Bake It Into Daily Life
Your playbook only works if your team uses it. The secret? Make it part of their daily routine.
- Train with It: Use the playbook during onboarding, mock calls, and role-play sessions.
- Reference It: During 1:1s, use it to troubleshoot issues. ("Let's check the objection-handling flowchart.")
- Track Adoption: Ask in weekly meetings: "Which section helped you this week?"

Developing a Scalable Playbook

Chapter 8: Frameworks and Processes

Example: SalesLoft's Living Playbook
Jeremy Donovan, SVP of Sales Strategy at SalesLoft, shares how they use their playbook to onboard new reps in half the usual time. By embedding customer stories, validated cadences, and objection-handling scripts directly into their CRM, they made the playbook an everyday tool—not just a one-time read.

Examples of Different Playbooks to Include in a Scalable BDR System
A single, sprawling playbook can become unwieldy. Instead, divide it into targeted playbooks that address specific aspects of your team's strategy and execution.

Here are essential playbooks to consider:

- **Competitor Playbook**
  Focus: Equip your team to handle competitive scenarios and position your solution effectively.
  - **Key Components:**
    - A comparison matrix outlining strengths and weaknesses of competitors relative to your product.
    - Objection-handling scripts tailored to common competitive challenges.
    - Messaging frameworks emphasizing your differentiators.

- **Persona Playbook**
  - **Focus**: Tailor messaging to specific buyer personas for maximum relevance.
  - **Key Components:**
    - Profiles highlighting roles, responsibilities, and decision-making criteria.
    - Pain points and priorities for each persona to inform outreach.
    - Adjusted messaging cadences and tone based on persona preferences.

- **Industry Playbook**
  - **Focus**: Adjust outreach and messaging to resonate with specific industries.
  - **Key Components:**
    - Trends and challenges unique to the industry.
    - Use cases and success stories demonstrating product value within the sector.
    - Industry-specific language and jargon to build credibility.

- **Role-Specific Playbook**
  - **Focus**: Personalize the approach based on job titles and responsibilities.
  - **Key Components:**
    - Insights into what matters most to individuals in specific roles.
    - Metrics and objectives that inform their decision-making.
    - Tactics for engaging them effectively in different stages of the buyer's journey.

Chapter 8: Frameworks and Processes

- **Regional Playbook**
    - **Focus**: Adapt strategies to suit geographic or cultural nuances.
    - **Key Components:**
        - Outreach preferences, including tone, timing, and formality, based on the region.
        - Regional regulations and compliance considerations.
        - Cultural insights to avoid missteps and enhance engagement.

Each of these playbooks works as a modular piece of a larger system, empowering your team to approach prospects with precision and relevance.

Key Takeaway
Building a playbook isn't about creating a static guide. It's about giving your team the tools to adapt, improve, and win consistently. Keep it simple, actionable, and alive. And remember—it's not about perfection; it's about progress.

Chapter 8: Frameworks and Processes

Integrating Technology into Your Workflow

Technology is the engine that drives modern BDR teams. The right tools amplify productivity, streamline processes, and provide actionable insights—but only if they're integrated thoughtfully. A disjointed tech stack can cause more headaches than it solves. This section focuses on building a cohesive workflow by effectively incorporating technology into your team's day-to-day operations.

Start with a Workflow Audit

Before adding or adjusting tools, map out your team's current workflow. Identify where technology enhances productivity and where gaps exist.

Key Questions to Ask:
- What processes are repetitive and ripe for automation?
- Where are inefficiencies slowing the team down?
- Which tools are essential, underutilized, or redundant?

Output: Create a simple flowchart showing how leads move through your system. Mark bottlenecks, inefficiencies, and areas where tools can help.

Build a Tech Stack for BDR Success

A well-rounded BDR tech stack should address the entire prospecting lifecycle, from research to outreach to reporting. Here are the must-have categories:

- **Prospecting and Research**
  - Tools that simplify finding and qualifying leads.
  - Features to prioritize: Contact information validation, company insights, and account scoring.
- **Outreach and Engagement**
  - Platforms that support multi-channel engagement (email, calls, LinkedIn).
  - Features to prioritize: Automated cadences, personalization capabilities, and call recording.
- **CRM (Customer Relationship Management)**
  - The central hub for tracking and managing leads.
  - Features to prioritize: Pipeline visibility, activity logging, and integration with other tools.
- **Analytics and Reporting**
  - Solutions that provide actionable insights into team performance.
  - Features to prioritize: Real-time dashboards, KPI tracking, and trend analysis.

Pro Tip: Avoid shiny new tools that don't address specific needs. Focus on tech that integrates seamlessly with your existing systems.

Integration Is Key

Even the best tools fail when they don't work together. Focus on creating a cohesive ecosystem where data flows smoothly across platforms.

Chapter 8: Frameworks and Processes

Key Steps for Integration:
- Centralize Your Data: Ensure all tools sync with your CRM to provide a single source of truth.
- Automate Data Entry: Reduce manual input by using tools that automatically log activities, such as emails and calls.
- Test for Compatibility: Before adding new tech, test its integration with your current stack to avoid siloed information.

- **Prioritize Ease of Use**
  - The best tools are the ones your team will actually use. Complex systems with steep learning curves often lead to resistance and underutilization.
  - How to Ensure Adoption:
  - Provide hands-on training and tutorials for every tool.
  - Gather team feedback before finalizing purchases to ensure the tool fits their needs.
  - Assign a tech champion on your team to troubleshoot and share tips.

- **Optimize Your Workflow with Automation**
  - Automation is a powerful ally, but only when balanced with the human touch. Over-automating can make interactions feel robotic.
  - Where to Automate:
  - Lead enrichment: Auto-populate contact details and firmographics in your CRM.
  - Outreach cadences: Automate follow-up sequences while allowing for manual personalization.
  - Reporting: Set up dashboards that auto-update to reflect performance metrics.

- **Monitor Performance and Adjust**
  - Your tech stack isn't static—it needs regular evaluation to ensure it continues to meet your team's needs.
  - Steps to Evaluate Effectiveness:
  - Conduct quarterly reviews of tool usage and ROI.
  - Monitor adoption rates: Are team members actively using the tools?
  - Survey the team: What's working? What feels clunky or redundant?

Comprehensive List of Tools for a Modern BDR Tech Stack

A high-performing BDR team requires a well-curated tech stack that combines battle-tested staples with next-generation disruptors. Together, they create an ecosystem that optimizes productivity, personalizes outreach, and drives results. Below is a categorized list tailored for every stage of the BDR workflow.

Chapter 8: Frameworks and Processes

- **Prospecting and Research Tools**
  Uncover insights about your prospects and find the right contacts to engage.
  - **Battle-Tested Staples:**
    - LinkedIn Sales Navigator: The ultimate tool for targeted lead discovery and relationship building.
    - ZoomInfo: Comprehensive contact data and company insights that have become an industry standard.
    - D&B Hoovers: Trusted for enterprise-level lead generation and in-depth firmographic details.
  - **Rising Powerhouses:**
    - Apollo.io: Combines data-driven prospecting with email automation in one seamless platform.
    - Lusha: Lightweight and efficient, offering verified contact details directly in your browser.
    - LeadIQ: Simplifies the prospecting workflow with CRM integrations and intuitive list-building.

- **Outreach and Engagement Tools**
  Engage prospects across multiple channels and scale your messaging without losing personalization.
  - **Battle-Tested Staples:**
    - Outreach.io: A cornerstone for managing sales sequences, calls, and tasks.
    - SalesLoft: Widely adopted for its multi-channel outreach capabilities and simplicity.
    - Yesware: A reliable tool for email tracking and follow-ups directly within your inbox.
  - **Rising Powerhouses:**
    - Regie.ai: Uses AI to create hyper-personalized email sequences at scale.
    - Vidyard: Perfect for video outreach, helping reps stand out in crowded inboxes.
    - Hyperise: Adds dynamic personalization elements, like customized images, to outreach efforts.

- **CRM (Customer Relationship Management)**
  Centralize all prospect and pipeline data in one place for streamlined tracking and collaboration.
  - Battle-Tested Staples:
    - Salesforce: The gold standard for robust CRM functionality, especially for large organizations.
    - HubSpot CRM: Ideal for teams seeking a user-friendly and scalable solution.
  - Rising Powerhouses:
    - Close: Designed for inside sales teams, with built-in calling and email features.

Chapter 8: Frameworks and Processes

- Pipedrive: Visual and intuitive, perfect for smaller teams or those needing simple pipeline management.

- **Call and Conversation Intelligence Tools**
  Gain deeper insights into sales calls and uncover patterns in successful interactions.
  - **Battle-Tested Staples:**
    - Gong.io: Renowned for its AI-powered analysis of sales calls, offering actionable insights.
    - Chorus.ai: Tracks call trends and helps teams refine their conversations to improve outcomes.
  - **Rising Powerhouses:**
    - Avoma: Combines call intelligence with collaborative meeting management.
    - Refract.ai: Focuses on coaching by analyzing conversation patterns and identifying skill gaps.

- **Intent Data Tools**
  Identify prospects who are actively in-market and ready to engage by using behavioral and intent data.
  - **Battle-Tested Staples:**
    - 6sense: Tracks intent signals across the buyer's journey to identify high-priority leads.
    - Demandbase: Integrates account-based marketing (ABM) with intent data to refine prospect targeting.
  - **Rising Powerhouses:**
    - Factors.ai: Provides intent data enriched with contextual insights to highlight warm leads.
    - Bombora: Offers company-level intent data to identify organizations actively researching topics relevant to your solution.

- **Personalization Tools**
  Add a human touch to outreach while maintaining the scale your team needs.
  - **Battle-Tested Staples:**
    - Hyperise: Inserts dynamic images and personalized content into email campaigns and LinkedIn messages.
    - Sendoso: Creates impactful touchpoints by sending customized gifts and direct mail.
  - **Rising Powerhouses:**
    - NiftyImages: Generates personalized visuals, such as countdown timers and unique images, to drive engagement.
    - Tella: Allows reps to record polished, personalized videos for higher prospect engagement.

Chapter 8: Frameworks and Processes

- **Automation and Workflow Tools**
    - Free your team from repetitive tasks and create efficient, scalable workflows.
  - **Battle-Tested Staples:**
    - Zapier: Connects your favorite apps to automate tedious processes.
    - Calendly: Simplifies meeting scheduling, reducing the back-and-forth.
  - **Rising Powerhouses:**
    - Clay: Automates lead sourcing and data enrichment with customizable workflows.
    - Cognism: Stands out for globally compliant data, particularly strong in EMEA and APAC regions.6. Data and Analytics Tools

- **Data & Analytics**
  Transform raw data into actionable insights to optimize team performance.
  - **Battle-Tested Staples:**
    - Google Analytics: Useful for tracking campaign performance and user engagement.
    - Tableau: A top choice for creating sophisticated data visualizations.
  - **Rising Powerhouses:**
    - Cumul.io: Lightweight and intuitive, ideal for building real-time dashboards.
    - Clari: Specializes in pipeline analytics and forecasting with AI-driven precision.

- **Email Warming Tools**
  Boost email deliverability and maintain sender reputation to land in inboxes, not spam folders.
  - **Battle-Tested Staples:**
    - Lemwarm (by Lemlist): Ensures your emails are trusted while seamlessly integrating into outreach campaigns.
    - Warmbox: Automates inbox warming with realistic back-and-forth interactions.
  - **Rising Powerhouses:**
    - Mailreach: Focused entirely on email warm-up, designed for teams scaling outreach volume.
    - GMass Warm: Tailored for Gmail users, warming email addresses while syncing with outreach tools.

By combining legacy staples like Salesforce and Outreach.io with newer tools like Clay and Hyperbound, you build a forward-thinking, adaptable tech stack. Each category works together to create a seamless, data-driven, and highly personalized BDR workflow.

Chapter 8: Frameworks and Processes

Automating for Efficiency Without Losing the Human Touch
Automation is your secret weapon as a BDR leader—it handles the grunt work so your team can focus on what really matters: building relationships and closing deals. But here's the catch: automation is like seasoning. Use too little, and everything feels bland and repetitive. Use too much, and it all tastes fake. The trick is to strike that perfect balance: efficient systems with enough personality to keep your outreach human.

Why Automation Is a Game-Changer
When done right, automation doesn't just save time; it turns your team into productivity ninjas. Think of all the time your reps spend entering data, crafting follow-ups, or manually updating CRMs. Now imagine all that done in the background.

Here's what automation brings to the table:
- **Task Mastery**: It zips through the tedious stuff—data entry, lead enrichment, scheduling—giving your reps hours back in their day.
- **Consistency for Days**: No more missed follow-ups or gaps in outreach. Automated cadences keep the machine humming.
- **Scale Without the Stress**: Want to double your prospecting efforts? Automation lets you grow without drowning your team in extra work.

Where to Automate (Without Killing the Vibe)
- **Lead Enrichment**: Stop wasting time Googling email addresses or company details. Tools like Clay and Lusha pull everything you need into your CRM faster than you can say "sales qualified lead."
- **Email Sequencing**: Use platforms like Outreach.io or SalesLoft to send automated follow-ups that feel personal. But leave space for custom touches—like a killer first line about their recent LinkedIn post.
- **CRM Updates**: Automate activity tracking (calls, emails, and meetings) to keep your CRM updated without making your reps feel like data-entry clerks.
- **Scheduling**: Tools like Calendly or Chili Piper let prospects pick meeting times themselves. No more "Does Tuesday at 3 work?" emails.

How to Keep It Personal
The fear with automation is that it makes you sound like a robot. Here's how to keep things real:
- **Add a Dash of You**: Personalize at least a sentence of every email that you send. Sure, automation sets up the sequence, but that custom opening line is what gets replies.
- **Know When to Step In**: Let automation do the heavy lifting, but don't send an email without giving it a quick once-over.
- **Get Creative:** Add videos with tools like Vidyard or Hyperise to stand out. It's still automated, but a smiling face (or a personalized GIF) goes a long way.

Chapter 8: Frameworks and Processes

Don't Go Overboard
Over-automation is like sending 20 identical LinkedIn connection requests—it screams "spam." Avoid these pitfalls:
- **Generic Cadences:** If your emails feel like they came from a template, they probably did. Automation should enhance your message, not erase its personality.
- **Siloed Data:** Tools that don't talk to each other create chaos. Make sure your stack plays nice (hello, integrations).
- **Skipping the Feedback Loop:** If something isn't working, tweak it. Automation isn't a "set it and forget it" game—it's more like "set it and improve it."

The Elephant in the Room: AI Agents and the Future of BDRs
There's no denying it—AI is the buzzword of the decade, and AI agents are poised to shake up the world of sales. From writing emails to booking meetings, these digital workhorses are already making waves. But here's the truth no one wants to admit: AI agents aren't here to replace BDRs; they're here to augment them.
Think of AI agents as the ultimate sidekick. Batman never worried about Robin stealing his thunder, right? Instead, they teamed up to fight crime more effectively. That's how you should approach AI: as a powerful partner that lets your team work smarter, not harder.

Why AI Agents Won't Replace BDRs
Let's start with what AI agents are great at:
- **Handling Repetitive Tasks:** AI thrives on predictable, repeatable processes. Lead enrichment, basic prospecting, scheduling—it's all child's play for a well-trained AI agent.
- **Scaling Outreach**: AI can craft and send hundreds of personalized emails faster than your fastest rep could type "Hi [First Name]."
- **Analyzing Data**: AI agents are masters of pattern recognition. They can identify which email templates, outreach cadences, or target industries are performing best in seconds.

But here's the kicker: AI can't replace the human touch. Building trust, understanding nuanced objections, and navigating complex buying committees require emotional intelligence and creativity—qualities that BDRs bring to the table.

How AI Agents Can Augment Your Team
Instead of fearing AI agents, embrace them as productivity boosters. Here's how they can elevate your BDRs:
- **Free Up Time for Strategy**: AI can handle mundane tasks like data entry or contact validation, leaving BDRs free to focus on creative problem-solving and strategic outreach.
- **Assist with Real-Time Insights**: During calls, AI tools like Gong or Wingman can provide live coaching tips, helping reps handle objections more effectively.

Automating for Efficiency Without Losing the Human Touch

Chapter 8: Frameworks and Processes

- **Automate Research**: AI agents can scour the web for relevant company news, recent funding rounds, or executive changes, feeding your reps actionable insights before they hit "send."
- **Supercharge Personalization**: Tools like Regie.ai or Hyperbound can create hyper-targeted email drafts based on prospect data, leaving reps to fine-tune the details for maximum impact.

Where AI Falls Short

AI agents might be smart, but they're not human. Here's what they still struggle with:

- **Complex Conversations:** AI can't read between the lines or adapt to unstructured dialogue the way a skilled BDR can.
- **Emotional Connection**: Prospects don't build relationships with algorithms—they build them with people. The warmth and authenticity of a human voice remain irreplaceable.
- **Strategic Thinking**: AI follows patterns and rules, but it can't innovate or think strategically to navigate unique challenges.

What This Means for BDR Teams

The rise of AI isn't a death knell for BDRs—it's a call to level up. Reps who embrace AI agents as collaborators rather than competitors will thrive. The future belongs to teams that blend the efficiency of AI with the creativity, empathy, and adaptability of human intelligence.

Here's how to position your team for success:

- Train your BDRs to work alongside AI tools, leveraging them for efficiency without losing sight of the personal touch.
- Reallocate time saved through automation to higher-value activities like deeper prospecting and relationship building.
- Foster a culture of adaptability, encouraging your team to embrace new tools and experiment with AI-driven strategies.

The Winning Formula: Humans + Technology

The best BDR teams of tomorrow won't be the ones that resist AI, nor the ones that over-rely on it. They'll be the teams that find the perfect synergy—using AI to handle the routine and amplifying human strengths to deliver real value.

The elephant in the room isn't whether AI will take over; it's whether BDRs will adapt. Spoiler alert: the smart ones will, and they'll be unstoppable.

Chapter 8: Frameworks and Processes

Ensuring Data Quality and Analytics

In the world of BDRs, data is king. The quality of your data and how well you use it can mean the difference between thriving and spinning your wheels. Yet, dirty data—outdated, incomplete, or inaccurate information—can derail even the most sophisticated workflows. On top of that, analytics without actionable insights is just noise. Let's talk about how to keep your data clean, actionable, and primed for results.

Why Data Quality Matters

Poor data impacts your team in three major ways:
- **Wasted Effort:** Reaching out to invalid emails or calling disconnected numbers frustrates reps and burns time.
- **Missed Opportunities:** Incomplete or inaccurate data might mean missing a warm lead ready to buy.
- **Eroded Trust:** When reps consistently encounter bad data, their confidence in your systems plummets—and that affects morale and productivity.

Great analytics start with great data. If your inputs are flawed, your outputs—like pipeline forecasts or conversion metrics—will be, too.

Key Pillars of Data Quality
- **Accuracy:** Ensure contact information, company details, and firmographics are correct and up-to-date.
- **Completeness:** Make sure all essential fields (like phone numbers, emails, and job titles) are filled in.
- **Consistency:** Standardize data formats across your CRM to avoid mismatched entries (e.g., using "VP" and "Vice President" interchangeably).
- **Timeliness:** Regularly update your data to account for job changes, company moves, or outdated information.

How to Ensure Clean Data
- **Automate Data Hygiene:** Use tools like ZoomInfo or Clay to enrich and verify records in real time. Automation reduces the chances of manual errors.
- **Schedule Regular Audits:** Set up quarterly or monthly data-cleaning routines to remove duplicates, update stale information, and fill in missing fields.
- **Integrate Data Sources:** Ensure all platforms (CRM, prospecting tools, email outreach systems) share data seamlessly to avoid discrepancies.
- **Empower Reps to Report Errors:** Build a culture where reps flag inaccurate data, creating a feedback loop that improves data quality over time.

Building an Analytics Framework That Drives Action

Analytics shouldn't just tell you what's happening—they should inform what to do next. A robust framework includes:
- **Real-Time Dashboards**: Use tools like Tableau or Clari to create intuitive dashboards that track team performance, pipeline health, and outreach

Chapter 8: Frameworks and Processes

metrics in real time.
- **Conversion Tracking:** Monitor metrics like email open rates, meeting-to-opportunity conversions, and pipeline contribution to identify bottlenecks.
- **Trend Analysis:** Look for patterns over time. For instance, if a certain industry consistently responds better to your outreach, double down on that vertical.
- **Rep Performance Metrics:** Track activity volume, response rates, and bookings at the individual level to identify coaching opportunities.

What to Measure in BDR Analytics
Your metrics should align with your goals. Here are the must-haves:
- **Activity Metrics**: Calls made, emails sent, LinkedIn connections requested.
- **Engagement Metrics:** Email reply rates, call connection rates, and meeting acceptance rates.
- **Pipeline Metrics:** Meetings booked, SQL (Sales-Qualified Lead) conversion rates, and pipeline contribution.
- **Win/Loss Analysis:** Insights into why opportunities convert—or don't—at each stage.

The Human Element in Data and Analytics
Even with automation and analytics tools, human oversight is essential. Data tells a story, but it's your team that interprets it and applies it to real-world strategies. Empower your BDRs to:
- **Question the Numbers:** Encourage reps to flag anomalies in data or metrics that don't align with their on-the-ground experience.
- **Act on Insights:** Train your team to use data-driven insights to refine their approach, like pivoting to a high-performing persona or experimenting with new cadences.

Closing Thought
Ensuring data quality and leveraging analytics isn't just a "nice-to-have" for modern BDR teams—it's a necessity. With clean data, actionable insights, and a culture of continuous improvement, your team can make smarter decisions, scale faster, and hit targets consistently.

Chapter 9: Leadership Best Practices

Leadership is the foundation of every high-performing BDR team. As a leader, you're not just managing people; you're inspiring them, guiding them through challenges, and setting the tone for success. This chapter is where we dig deep into the skills, strategies, and philosophies that separate good leaders from transformative ones.

Let's dive into the first topic.

Coaching: When to Nudge, When to Push

If you're leading a team that includes Gen Z reps, you've probably noticed they approach work differently. Raised in the age of rapid technological advances, social media, and a greater emphasis on mental health, Gen Z isn't your typical workforce. But here's the good news: they bring adaptability, purpose-driven thinking, and creativity to the table. Coaching Gen Z requires you to fine-tune how and when to nudge versus push because their motivations, expectations, and work styles are uniquely their own.

Why Gen Z Is Different

- **Purpose over Paychecks:** Gen Z craves meaning in their work. They want to know how their efforts contribute to the team and the larger mission.
- **Feedback Obsessed:** They grew up in a world of likes, comments, and instant feedback. Gen Z expects regular check-ins and guidance, not once-a-quarter reviews.
- **Tech-Savvy but People-Centric:** While they're comfortable with automation and digital tools, they value genuine human connection in the workplace.
- **Mental Health Matters:** Burnout is a big red flag for Gen Z. They're willing to work hard but won't stick around if it feels unsustainable.

How to Nudge Gen Z Reps

Nudging works well with Gen Z because they value autonomy and learning. A nudge lets them explore solutions without feeling micromanaged.

- **Guide, Don't Dictate:** Frame coaching moments as collaborative problem-solving rather than directives. For instance, "Let's brainstorm together how you might approach this prospect differently."
- **Show the Big Picture:** Tie individual actions to team or company-wide goals. For example, "When you hit your outreach goals, it directly impacts the pipeline health for the entire sales team."
- **Micro-Milestones:** Gen Z thrives on small, measurable progress. Break long-term goals into shorter, attainable steps so they can see their growth in real time.
- **Peer-to-Peer Coaching:** Gen Z reps often value insights from their peers. Pair them with high-performing team members to share strategies.

When and How to Push Gen Z

While Gen Z thrives on encouragement, they're hungry for growth and challenge. Pushing, when done with care, can energize them to reach new heights.

Chapter 9: Leadership Best Practices

- **Challenge Their Comfort Zone:** Gen Z wants to grow, but they might hesitate to take on something that feels unfamiliar or risky. Push by framing new challenges as opportunities: "I think you're ready to handle enterprise accounts. Let's work together to map out your first few outreach strategies."
- **Be Transparent**: If performance is slipping, be direct but empathetic. Avoid vague critiques like "you're not working hard enough." Instead, say, "Your meeting-to-pipeline conversion rate has dropped. Let's figure out what's going on and build a plan to get it back up."
- **Tie Growth to Their Personal Values:** For Gen Z, it's not just about climbing the ladder. Connect challenges to their purpose. For example, "Taking on this account will sharpen your negotiation skills, which will make you an even stronger candidate for leadership roles in the future."

The Fine Line Between Motivation and Burnout
Gen Z is deeply aware of burnout culture, and as a leader, you need to push without tipping them over the edge.
- **Recognize Signs of Burnout Early:** Watch for disengagement, decreased performance, or frustration in their tone during calls or meetings.
- **Balance Accountability with Empathy:** When pushing, acknowledge the effort they're putting in and express confidence in their ability to handle it.
- **Encourage Breaks:** Let them know it's okay to pause and recharge. For example, "You've been crushing your targets, but I want to make sure you're not overloading yourself. Take some time to reset if you need it."

Practical Coaching Tips for Gen Z Reps
- **Ask Questions Instead of Giving Answers:** "What do you think your next step should be?" opens the door for self-driven solutions.
- **Use Stories to Connect:** Share your own experiences of overcoming similar challenges to create relatability.
- **Provide Quick Feedback Loops:** Gen Z values speed—don't wait for a formal 1:1. A Slack message with quick praise or constructive tips goes a long way.
- **Celebrate Growth, Not Just Results:** Highlight the effort they're putting in, even if the outcome isn't perfect.

Closing Thought
Coaching Gen Z isn't about reinventing the wheel—it's about meeting them where they are. Whether you're nudging them to build confidence or pushing them to tackle big goals, the key is to tailor your approach to their strengths, values, and work style. When done right, Gen Z reps aren't just another team member; they're a force of innovation and creativity that will take your team to the next level.

Chapter 9: Leadership Best Practices

Building Trust and Accountability: The Backbone of Leadership
Trust and accountability are the glue that hold any high-performing team together, but with Gen Z in the mix, they take on a new level of importance. This generation doesn't blindly follow authority—they demand authenticity, transparency, and fairness. They want to work for leaders they respect and believe in, and they'll show up for those who show up for them.

For leaders, this means creating an environment where trust is earned and accountability isn't about finger-pointing—it's about mutual growth and shared goals.

How to Build Trust with Your Team
- **Start with Transparency:** Gen Z thrives in environments where leaders are open and honest. Whether it's explaining the reasoning behind a new quota or admitting when you don't have all the answers, being real fosters respect.
- **Be Consistent:** Trust is built through consistent actions. Follow through on your promises—whether it's a scheduled 1:1, delivering feedback, or advocating for their needs with upper management.
- **Make Trust a Two-Way Street:** Trust isn't a one-sided game. Give your team the autonomy to own their tasks and make decisions. Micromanagement kills trust faster than any bad policy.
- **Lead with Empathy:** Take the time to understand their challenges—both professional and personal. For example, if a BDR is struggling to hit their metrics, dig deeper: Are they facing burnout? Are there gaps in their training?

How Accountability Looks in the Gen Z Era
Gen Z doesn't shy away from accountability, but they don't respond well to outdated models of top-down management. For them, accountability is about collaboration and fairness.
- **Set Clear Expectations:** Ambiguity breeds frustration. Ensure every team member knows what's expected of them—whether it's KPIs, communication standards, or project deadlines.
- **Create a Culture of Ownership:** Empower your team to take responsibility for their wins and misses. Instead of focusing on blame when things go wrong, focus on what can be learned and improved.
- **Celebrate Accountability:** When someone steps up to take responsibility—especially for a mistake—acknowledge it positively. This shows that accountability is about growth, not punishment.

Trust and Accountability in Action
Let's say you've rolled out a new prospecting strategy. Here's how trust and accountability play into its success:
- **Building Trust:** Share the "why" behind the strategy, explaining how it aligns with broader goals. Openly admit that it's a test and that tweaks might be necessary based on their feedback.

Chapter 9: Leadership Best Practices

- **Fostering Accountability:** Set clear targets for each rep, but frame them as team goals rather than individual mandates. Check in weekly to review progress and invite suggestions for improvement.

By involving the team in the process, you show trust in their abilities while holding them accountable for results.

Navigating Challenges Without Breaking Trust
Even in a culture of trust and accountability, conflicts and challenges are inevitable. Here's how to handle them with grace:
- **Address Issues Early:** Whether it's a missed deadline or a misstep in outreach, tackle it as soon as possible. Waiting too long can make it harder to resolve without resentment.
- **Separate the Person from the Problem:** Focus on the behavior, not the individual. For example, instead of saying, "You're too disorganized," try, "Let's look at ways to streamline your prospecting workflow."
- **Model Accountability:** If a strategy or directive from you doesn't work, own it. Saying, "I miscalculated the target expectations this quarter" builds trust and shows your team that accountability starts at the top.

What Gen Z Expects from Leaders
Gen Z holds their leaders to high standards, and that's a good thing. They want leaders who:
- **Inspire, Not Intimidate:** Forget command-and-control leadership. Gen Z responds to leaders who motivate through vision and shared purpose.
- **Are Accessible:** They value leaders who are approachable and willing to listen. Regular check-ins and open-door policies go a long way.
- **Champion Fairness:** Gen Z has a strong sense of justice. Treating everyone equitably and recognizing contributions fairly are non-negotiables.

Practical Tips for Leaders
- **Trust First:** Trust is built through actions, but don't wait for someone to "prove" themselves. Give trust freely, and you'll see it reciprocated.
- **Regular Check-Ins:** Hold consistent 1:1s to align on expectations, provide feedback, and build rapport.
- **Collaborate on Solutions:** When addressing accountability issues, involve the team member in crafting a solution. This builds buy-in and ensures the plan is actionable.
- **Be Transparent About Your Decisions:** Whether it's assigning accounts or setting new goals, explain your rationale. Transparency eliminates speculation and fosters trust.

Chapter 9: Leadership Best Practices

Communication Skills That Inspire Action

Leadership isn't just about having a vision—it's about bringing that vision to life through the way you communicate. Words have power, and as a BDR leader, your communication style can either inspire your team to thrive or leave them feeling stuck and disengaged. For Gen Z in particular, communication needs to be authentic, clear, and inclusive. This generation doesn't respond to corporate jargon or top-down directives—they crave connection, purpose, and dialogue.

Let's explore how you can communicate in a way that motivates action and fosters growth.

What Gen Z Expects from Communication
- **Clarity is Key:** Gen Z values transparency and directness. They don't want to decode vague instructions or sit through meetings filled with buzzwords.
- **Collaboration Over Commands:** This is a generation that grew up valuing teamwork and inclusivity. They expect leaders to involve them in decisions and encourage their input.
- **Purpose-Driven Messaging:** Gen Z isn't motivated by "because I said so" leadership. They want to understand the "why" behind tasks and decisions.
- **Digital Fluency:** With Gen Z, communication isn't just verbal—it's Slack messages, video calls, and shared docs. Adapt to their digital-first style while maintaining the human touch.

How to Communicate with Impact
- **Paint the Big Picture:**
  - Every task, no matter how small, should feel like part of a larger purpose. Instead of saying, "Send 50 follow-up emails today," try, "Each follow-up email gets us one step closer to hitting our team goal of $1M in pipeline this quarter." Connecting daily tasks to larger objectives gives meaning to the grind.
- **Be Authentic:**
  - Drop the "manager voice." Your team wants to hear the real you—flaws, humor, and all. Authenticity builds trust and makes your communication relatable.
- **Make Feedback a Conversation:**
  - Gone are the days of one-sided feedback sessions. When giving feedback, ask questions like, "How do you feel about your progress this month?" or "What could I do to support you better?" These questions show that you value their perspective and create a two-way dialogue.
- **Adapt Your Style:**
  - Not every team member processes information the same way. Some may thrive on face-to-face meetings, while others prefer written instructions. Take the time to understand how each person communicates best.
- **Use Stories to Inspire:**
  - A well-told story can drive home a point better than a dozen data points.

Chapter 9: Leadership Best Practices

- Share anecdotes about your own experiences or highlight a team member's success story. For example: "I remember when I struggled with objection handling. Here's what worked for me—and I see the same potential in you."

Communication Channels That Work for Gen Z
- **Slack and Messaging Tools:** Keep updates concise and actionable. Avoid flooding channels with unnecessary information—Gen Z values brevity.
- **1:1 Meetings:** Use these as a chance to build rapport, offer tailored feedback, and align on goals. Keep them collaborative and avoid dominating the conversation.
- **Video Messages:** For announcements or important updates, a quick video can be more engaging than an email. Tools like Loom make it easy to record and share.
- **Recognition Platforms:** Gen Z thrives on recognition, but a simple "good job" won't cut it. Highlight specific achievements in team Slack channels or during meetings to make praise feel meaningful.

Dealing with Difficult Conversations
Sometimes, communication involves delivering tough messages. Here's how to approach difficult conversations with grace and effectiveness:

- **Be Honest, Not Harsh:** Gen Z values transparency, but how you deliver the message matters. Lead with empathy and focus on solutions rather than just pointing out problems.
- **Start with Positives**: Begin by acknowledging what the individual is doing well. This sets a constructive tone for the discussion.
- **Collaborate on Solutions**: Instead of dictating next steps, ask, "What do you think we could do to turn this around?" Co-creating solutions fosters accountability and engagement.
- **Follow Up:** After a tough conversation, check in a few days later to see how they're doing. This shows you care about their growth, not just their performance metrics.

Real-World Example
Brian Halligan, co-founder of HubSpot, attributes much of the company's success to its culture of "radical candor." At HubSpot, leaders are trained to be direct but compassionate, ensuring feedback is actionable and tied to personal and company growth. This approach has not only inspired better performance but also earned the company recognition as one of the best places to work for younger generations.

Practical Tips for Inspiring Communication
- **End Every Conversation with Clarity**: Summarize key takeaways and next steps to avoid confusion.

Chapter 9: Leadership Best Practices

- **Overcommunicate in Uncertainty:** When big changes are happening, share frequent updates to keep your team informed and grounded.
- **Celebrate Wins Loudly:** Whether it's a Slack shoutout or a team-wide email, make recognition public and specific.
- **Inject Humor When Appropriate:** A little lightheartedness can make even stressful situations more manageable.

Closing Thought

Great communication isn't about talking at your team—it's about talking with them. By being clear, authentic, and empathetic, you can inspire action, build trust, and create a culture where every team member feels heard and valued.

Chapter 9: Leadership Best Practices

Dealing with Conflicts Like a Pro

Conflict is inevitable when you're managing a team of ambitious, diverse, and opinionated individuals. Whether it's friction between team members, disagreements over strategy, or performance issues, how you handle conflicts can either strengthen your team's dynamics or sow division.

For leaders, especially those working with Gen Z, managing conflict is about more than resolving issues—it's about fostering a culture of open dialogue, mutual respect, and continuous improvement. Let's explore how to approach conflicts head-on without losing momentum (or your cool).

Understanding the Nature of Conflicts
Conflicts in a BDR team often arise from:
- Misaligned Expectations: When goals or roles aren't clearly defined, frustration builds.
- Communication Breakdowns: A lack of clarity or tone misinterpretations, especially in digital communication, can spark unnecessary tensions.
- Performance Discrepancies: Uneven workloads or perceived unfairness can lead to resentment.
- Personality Clashes: Different working styles or attitudes sometimes clash, especially in a high-pressure environment.

Recognizing the root cause of conflict is the first step in resolving it effectively.

How to Handle Conflicts Gracefully
Address Issues Early:
Letting conflicts fester is a recipe for escalation. As soon as you notice friction, step in to mediate. For example, if two team members aren't collaborating effectively, have a one-on-one with each to understand their perspectives before bringing them together to resolve the issue.

Separate Emotions from Issues:
When emotions are high, it's easy for conflicts to spiral. Stay calm and focus on the facts. For instance, instead of saying, "You're always late to meetings," try, "I've noticed you've been late to our last three team meetings. Let's talk about what's going on."

Encourage Open Dialogue:
Create a safe space for team members to voice their concerns without fear of judgment. Use neutral language like, "I'd love to hear your perspective on what happened," to invite honesty.

Facilitate Collaboration:
Conflict resolution isn't about "winning" or "losing"—it's about finding common ground. Encourage team members to co-create solutions. For example, "How can we divide this project in a way that feels fair to both of you?"

Be Decisive When Necessary:
Not all conflicts can or should be resolved collaboratively. If a decision is needed to

Chapter 9: Leadership Best Practices

move forward, be firm but fair. Explain your reasoning transparently to maintain trust.

The Gen Z Factor in Conflict Resolution
Gen Z's approach to conflict often differs from older generations. They value directness but expect empathy. Here's how to tailor your approach:
- **Be Transparent:** If you're mediating a conflict, explain your role and what you hope to achieve. For example, "My goal here is to ensure both of you feel heard and that we find a path forward together."
- **Acknowledge Emotional Responses:** Gen Z doesn't shy away from expressing frustration or disappointment. Validate their feelings without letting emotions dominate the discussion.
- **Focus on Growth:** Frame conflicts as opportunities to learn. "This disagreement has highlighted some gaps in our process. Let's use it as a chance to improve how we collaborate."

What to Avoid During Conflict Resolution
- **Taking Sides:** Even if one party seems more "right," your role is to remain neutral and solution-focused.
- **Delaying Action:** Procrastination sends the message that the issue isn't important.
- **Overreacting:** If you escalate alongside the conflict, you'll lose credibility as a calming, effective leader.

Pro Tips for Handling Conflicts Like a Pro
- Practice Active Listening: Repeat back what you hear to show you understand, and ask clarifying questions to get to the root of the issue.
- Set Clear Boundaries: If a conflict turns personal or disrespectful, step in immediately to re-establish professional norms.
- Follow Up: Check in with the parties involved after resolving the issue to ensure the solution is working and no lingering tensions remain.

Using Humor to Diffuse Tension
A well-timed lighthearted comment can break the ice in heated situations. For example, if a meeting gets tense, a simple, "Wow, I think we all need a coffee refill after this one!" can help reset the tone. Be careful to use humor appropriately—make sure it's inclusive and doesn't undermine the seriousness of the issue.

Closing Thought
Conflict is inevitable, but it doesn't have to be destructive. When approached with empathy, transparency, and a focus on growth, conflicts can strengthen your team and improve how you work together. Leaders who handle conflict with grace set the tone for a resilient, collaborative culture that thrives under pressure.

Chapter 9: Leadership Best Practices

Handling Challenges with Grace (or at Least Humor)

Leadership isn't just about steering the ship when the waters are calm—it's about navigating storms with composure and keeping morale high when things don't go as planned. Challenges are inevitable in any BDR team, from missed targets to team conflicts or sudden market changes. How you handle these moments defines your leadership and sets the tone for how your team responds.

Grace is about staying grounded, while humor helps keep things in perspective. Let's dive into strategies for tackling challenges in a way that inspires your team, even when the going gets tough.

Why Grace Matters in Leadership

Challenges can amplify stress and uncertainty, especially for a Gen Z-heavy team that values transparency, empathy, and purpose. Leading with grace means:

- Remaining Calm Under Pressure: When your team sees you handling a crisis with confidence, they're more likely to stay focused and engaged.
- Fostering Trust: Showing composure reassures your team that you've got their back, even in difficult situations.
- Encouraging Resilience: Your attitude sets the example for how challenges should be approached—as opportunities to learn and grow.

Injecting Humor (Without Undermining the Seriousness)

Humor isn't about making light of serious problems—it's about diffusing tension and creating an environment where people feel safe addressing challenges head-on.

- **Break the Ice:** A well-timed joke or quip can ease anxiety. For instance, if targets are missed, saying, "Well, at least we're consistent—we missed by exactly the same amount as last quarter!" can shift the mood without downplaying the issue.
- **Keep It Inclusive:** Avoid sarcasm or humor that could alienate team members. Humor should unify, not divide.
- **Humanize Yourself:** Share a relatable anecdote about a time you made a mistake or faced a similar challenge. For example, "I remember my first quarter as a BDR manager—we missed quota, and I accidentally blamed the CRM for losing data. Spoiler alert: It was user error."

Leading Through Tough Times
Be Transparent About Challenges:
Your team doesn't need every detail, but they do need clarity. If there's a tough quarter ahead, be honest about the challenges and your plan to navigate them. For example, "The market is tight right now, but we're doubling down on targeting industries that are still growing."

Chapter 9: Leadership Best Practices

Reframe the Situation:
Help your team see challenges as opportunities. Instead of saying, "We're behind on quota," reframe it as, "This is a chance to rethink our approach and experiment with new outreach strategies."

Empower Problem-Solving:
Involve the team in finding solutions. For example, during a pipeline slowdown, ask, "What have you noticed in your outreach? Are there industries or tactics that seem to be working better than others?" This not only fosters collaboration but also builds confidence.

Celebrate Small Wins:
During challenging times, it's easy to focus on what's going wrong. Instead, spotlight small victories to keep morale up. Acknowledge every booked meeting, positive email reply, or completed cadence.

How Gen Z Responds to Leadership in Tough Times
Gen Z craves authenticity, and they'll see through anything that feels forced or disingenuous. Here's how to align your approach with their expectations:
- Acknowledge Their Efforts: Even when results are lagging, recognize the hard work your team is putting in.
- Ask for Input: Gen Z values collaboration. Show them their voices matter by involving them in decision-making.
- Focus on Growth: Frame challenges as opportunities for skill-building and innovation. For example, "This is a tough market, but it's a great chance to sharpen our multi-threading skills."

Pro Tips for Handling Challenges with Grace (and Humor)
- **Stay Accessible:** Make yourself available for questions and concerns. During tough times, visibility is key to maintaining trust.
- **Practice Emotional Agility:** Acknowledge your own feelings without letting them overwhelm you. Share, "This is a tough moment, but I'm confident we'll get through it together."
- **Use Humor Sparingly:** Think of humor as a seasoning, not the main course. Use it to diffuse tension, not distract from the issue at hand.
- **Focus on Solutions, Not Blame:** Lead problem-solving discussions with an optimistic tone, asking, "What can we do differently to move forward?"

Closing Thought
Handling challenges with grace and humor is about creating an environment where your team feels supported, even when things don't go as planned. When you lead with authenticity, empathy, and a touch of lightheartedness, you not only navigate tough times effectively—you also build a team that's more resilient, engaged, and ready to tackle whatever comes next.

Chapter 10: Measuring Success

In leadership, measuring success isn't just about hitting quotas or tracking numbers. Success is multi-dimensional, especially for BDR teams, where metrics must capture both outcomes and behaviors. By balancing leading and lagging indicators, leaders can paint a fuller picture of team performance while also predicting future results.

This topic goes beyond the usual dashboards to explore everything from emotional indicators to predictive analytics. Let's dive deep.

Leading vs. Lagging Indicators: A Comprehensive Guide for BDR Leaders

Measuring success as a BDR leader goes beyond tracking what has already happened. It's about understanding what's happening now and predicting what's coming next. This is where leading and lagging indicators come into play. Both are essential, but they serve very different purposes. The challenge is to not just measure them, but to act on them effectively to drive sustainable success.
Let's break down how to interpret and respond to these indicators with actionable strategies.

Dealing with Lagging Indicators

Lagging indicators, such as meetings booked or pipeline contribution, provide a clear snapshot of past performance. They're critical for understanding whether your team is hitting targets and achieving desired outcomes. However, lagging indicators are reactive—they tell you what's already happened but not why or how to fix issues.

Steps to Address Lagging Indicators:

- **Identify Trends:** Look for patterns across reporting periods. Are numbers consistently improving, stagnant, or declining? Trends offer valuable clues about underlying causes.
- **Dive Deeper:** Lagging indicators are surface-level metrics. If meetings booked are down, dig into associated data like response rates, show rates, or account targeting to uncover root causes.
- **Set a Baseline:** Establish benchmarks for key metrics so you can contextualize performance. For example, a 10% drop in pipeline contribution is concerning only if it deviates significantly from historical trends or industry standards.
- **Communicate Transparently:** When lagging indicators show issues, address them directly with your team. For instance, "We're 20% behind on meetings booked this quarter. Let's analyze what's slowing us down and adjust our approach together."

Action Plan for Lagging Indicators:

- If pipeline contribution is declining: Reevaluate lead quality and identify bottlenecks in the funnel. Are leads getting stuck at the qualification stage?

Chapter 10: Measuring Success

- If quota attainment is low: Analyze individual performance to determine if the issue is widespread or concentrated with certain reps. Tailor coaching accordingly.
- If SQL-to-close ratios are dropping: Collaborate with sales to ensure proper follow-up and alignment on lead quality expectations.

Dealing with Leading Indicators

Leading indicators act as your early-warning system. They reveal the actions and behaviors that predict future outcomes. These metrics are your opportunity to course-correct before issues escalate.

Steps to Act on Leading Indicators:

- **Monitor Consistently:** Unlike lagging indicators, leading metrics require frequent checks. Daily or weekly reviews ensure you catch problems early.
- **Define Key Activities:** Identify the most impactful actions for your team. For example, if calls made per day correlate strongly with meetings booked, prioritize this activity.
- **Set Incremental Goals:** Leading indicators work best when paired with smaller, manageable targets. Instead of aiming for 100 calls a week, challenge reps to increase their volume by 10% over the next few days.
- **Focus on Quality, Not Just Quantity:** High activity levels don't guarantee success. Track qualitative metrics like personalized messaging in emails or effective objection handling during calls.
- **Provide Immediate Feedback:** Leading indicators offer a chance to intervene quickly. For example, if response rates are dropping, review email templates or cadence timing with the team and adjust immediately.

Action Plan for Leading Indicators:

- **If activity volume is declining:** Introduce gamification or incentives to reignite motivation and track engagement.
- **If response rates are low:** Test new CTAs, messaging angles, or personalization techniques. A/B testing can help pinpoint what resonates best.
- **If meeting show rates are inconsistent:** Reinforce the importance of confirmation emails or adjust your scheduling tools to include reminders.

Addressing Emotional Indicators

While data metrics are essential, emotional indicators offer insights into team morale, confidence, and energy levels—critical factors that directly impact performance.

Steps to Interpret and Improve Emotional Indicators:

- **Pulse Check Surveys:** Use tools or informal check-ins to gauge morale. Questions like, "How confident do you feel in hitting your targets this week?" or "What's your biggest roadblock right now?" can reveal underlying issues.

Chapter 10: Measuring Success

- One-on-Ones: Regular individual conversations are invaluable for understanding emotional dynamics. Listen carefully to concerns and provide actionable support.
- Acknowledge Stress Points: If energy levels seem low, openly acknowledge the team's workload. For example, "I know it's been a tough week with high activity targets. Let's take a breather and reassess what's most important."
- Celebrate Wins: Even small victories can boost morale. Make it a habit to recognize achievements during team meetings or on internal communication channels.

Action Plan for Emotional Indicators:
- **If morale is low:** Organize a team-building fun activity to reset the energy. Reinforce that setbacks are part of the process and focus on long-term wins.
- **If confidence is wavering:** Invest in additional training or provide quick-win opportunities, like targeting low-hanging fruit leads to rebuild momentum.
- **If interpersonal dynamics are strained:** Address conflicts early with open dialogue and mediation to maintain team cohesion.

How to Balance Leading, Lagging, and Emotional Indicators

Success isn't measured by one type of metric alone—it's about connecting the dots between all three:
- Correlate Indicators: If activity volume (leading) is high, but pipeline contribution (lagging) is low, emotional indicators like confidence or morale might explain the gap.
- Adjust Weekly Priorities: Use leading indicators to set weekly goals, monitor emotional indicators to gauge team readiness, and review lagging indicators to track overall progress.
- Involve the Team: Share leading and lagging metrics openly, and invite your team to contribute ideas for improvement. This fosters accountability and collaboration.

Practical Tools to Manage Indicators
- **Dashboards**: Use tools like Salesforce or HubSpot to centralize leading and lagging metrics for real-time tracking.
- **Analytics Platforms:** Advanced platforms like Clari can help forecast future outcomes based on leading indicators.
- **Surveys:** Implement tools like Officevibe or a simple Google Form to measure morale and confidence on a regular basis.

Blending Data and Emotional Indicators

To lead effectively, you need to look beyond the numbers. Combining quantitative metrics (data indicators) with qualitative insights (emotional indicators) gives you a fuller picture of what's happening with your team and why. This holistic approach helps you spot patterns, identify root causes, and implement targeted solutions.

Leading vs. Lagging Indicators

Chapter 10: Measuring Success

Example 1: High Activity, Low Confidence
- Scenario: A rep's activity volume is high—they're making calls, sending emails, and hitting their outreach targets. However, during one-on-ones, they express doubts about the quality of their efforts, and their tone feels uncertain.
- Indicators:
    - Data: High activity (leading indicator).
    - Emotion: Low confidence (emotional indicator).
- Action: Review their recent outreach results and offer constructive feedback. Share scripts or templates that have worked for others, and highlight small wins to boost their confidence. For instance, "Your last email sequence had a 20% open rate—that's a strong starting point. Let's tweak the CTA and see if we can improve the reply rate."

Example 2: Low Response Rates, Rising Frustration
- Scenario: The team's response rates are dropping week over week, and you notice frustration during meetings. Reps are starting to blame "bad leads" or "tough markets."
- Indicators:
    - Data: Low response rates (leading indicator).
    - Emotion: Rising frustration (emotional indicator).
- Action: Acknowledge their feelings, then refocus the discussion on solutions. Introduce A/B testing for subject lines or experiment with new outreach cadences. Reinforce the idea that setbacks are part of experimentation, saying, "Every low response rate is a data point. Let's use it to refine and get stronger."

Example 3: Strong Pipeline, Low Energy
- Scenario: Your pipeline metrics look healthy, but in team meetings, energy levels are noticeably low. Reps seem disengaged and quieter than usual.
- Indicators:
    - Data: Strong pipeline contribution (lagging indicator).
    - Emotion: Low energy (emotional indicator).
- Action: Burnout could be the culprit. Encourage your team to take breaks and balance their workload. Reframe upcoming challenges as exciting opportunities, and introduce a lighter activity, such as a team lunch or a friendly competition, to lift spirits.

Example 4: Stalled Conversions, Waning Morale
- Scenario: SQL-to-close ratios are stagnating, and morale is slipping. Reps are hesitant to pass leads to sales, citing doubts about lead quality.
- Indicators:
    - Data: Low SQL-to-close ratio (lagging indicator).
    - Emotion: Waning morale (emotional indicator).

Action: Collaborate with the sales team to realign on what qualifies as an SQL. Provide coaching to rebuild reps' confidence to identify strong leads.

Chapter 10: Measuring Success

Communicate openly, saying, "Your instincts are key to this process. Let's refine our criteria and make this smoother for everyone."

Example 5: High Show Rates, Growing Enthusiasm
- Scenario: Meeting show rates are climbing, and team enthusiasm is contagious. Reps are volunteering to share their successful strategies during meetings.
- Indicators:
  - Data: High show rates (leading indicator).
  - Emotion: Growing enthusiasm (emotional indicator).
- Action: Build on this momentum by encouraging collaboration. Ask top performers to host micro-training sessions for their peers. Reinforce their efforts by publicly celebrating the wins. For example, "This 90% show rate is phenomenal—it's clear your personalization tactics are making an impact."

Why Blending Indicators Works
By combining data and emotional indicators, you move beyond superficial observations to uncover the deeper dynamics at play. This allows you to:
- Predict Performance Trends: Emotional indicators often reveal performance risks before data does.
- Address Root Causes: Instead of reacting to surface-level metrics, you'll tackle the underlying issues driving them.
- Build a Resilient Team: Paying attention to emotional health ensures your team can sustain success, even under pressure.

Closing the Loop
Indicators are only as useful as the actions they inspire. Leading indicators give you a chance to prevent issues before they snowball, while lagging indicators help you measure success and refine strategies. Emotional indicators fill in the gaps, providing a deeper understanding of your team's overall health. The best leaders don't just track metrics—they use them to drive meaningful, lasting change.

Chapter 10: Measuring Success

Reviewing Team and Individual Performance

Performance reviews are often viewed as formalities, but for BDR leaders, they're critical touchpoints to align, motivate, and grow your team. When done well, performance reviews go beyond "what happened" to uncover "why it happened" and "what's next." For Gen Z team members, who thrive on regular feedback and purpose-driven discussions, traditional annual reviews won't cut it. They expect a more dynamic and collaborative process.

Let's explore how to review performance effectively, blending data, insights, and coaching to drive both individual and team success.

What Effective Performance Reviews Should Accomplish

- **Clarity**: Provide reps with a clear understanding of where they stand and what's expected of them.
- **Growth**: Highlight areas for improvement and opportunities for skill development.
- **Motivation**: Reinforce their contributions and tie their efforts to team and company goals.
- **Alignment**: Ensure individual goals are aligned with broader organizational objectives.

Building a Performance Review Framework

Preparation Is Key:
Gather relevant metrics and examples to make reviews actionable and grounded in reality. Consider:

- Individual KPIs: Activity volume, response rates, meetings booked, pipeline contribution.
- Qualitative Feedback: Observations from role-playing sessions, call reviews, or peer feedback.
- Emotional Indicators: Morale, energy, and confidence levels based on check-ins and behavior.

Structure the Review:

- Start with Strengths: Open with what's going well to set a positive tone.
- Dive into Data: Present key metrics and connect them to behaviors or strategies.
- Discuss Areas for Improvement: Be clear, constructive, and specific about what needs to change.
- Collaborate on Goals: Co-create action plans for the next quarter or sprint, focusing on both performance and development.

Reviewing Team Performance

A team-level review ensures everyone understands how their collective efforts impact the organization. It also helps identify systemic challenges or opportunities.

Chapter 10: Measuring Success

How to Conduct a Team Review:
- **Celebrate Wins:** Highlight key successes, such as record-breaking months or improved conversion rates. Be specific about the strategies that worked.
- **Share Metrics Transparently:** Use dashboards to show aggregate activity, engagement, and pipeline metrics.
- **Identify Trends:** For example, "Response rates have been trending down across industries. Let's discuss why this might be happening and brainstorm solutions."
- **Reinforce Collaboration:** Recognize team members who exemplified teamwork, such as sharing effective scripts or helping colleagues improve.

Reviewing Individual Performance

Individual reviews are where you dig into personalized feedback and development plans. Here's how to ensure they're productive and motivating:

- **Be Data-Driven:**
  Start with the numbers, but don't stop there. For example, "Your meeting show rate was 85%, which is excellent. What do you think is driving that success?" Use this as a springboard to reinforce strong behaviors.
- **Focus on Specifics:**
  Avoid vague feedback like "You need to work harder." Instead, say, "Your email response rates dropped to 10% this month. Let's review your messaging together to identify improvements."
- **Tie Efforts to Goals:**
  Connect their actions to broader objectives. For instance, "Your outreach volume directly contributed to the team hitting our pipeline goal this quarter. That's a big win for all of us."
- **Discuss Development:**
  Ask, "What skills do you want to build in the next quarter?" This opens the door for coaching opportunities, training sessions, or mentorship connections.

Real-Time Feedback vs. Formal Reviews

Gen Z thrives on regular, bite-sized feedback rather than waiting for formal reviews. Balance the two by integrating:

- **Weekly 1:1s:** Use these for short-term goal check-ins and quick course corrections.
- **Monthly Performance Snapshots:** Share a summary of key metrics and observations to keep progress visible.
- **Quarterly Reviews:** Dive deeper into patterns, behaviors, and long-term development plans.

How to Handle Underperformance
Address It Early:
The longer you wait, the harder it is to course-correct. Start the conversation as soon as you notice issues, saying, "I've noticed your activity volume has dropped recently. Let's discuss what's going on."

Chapter 10: Measuring Success

Focus on Behaviors, Not Personalities:
Frame feedback around actions: "The current cadence isn't yielding results. Let's test a new approach together."

Collaborate on a Plan:
Involve the rep in creating an improvement plan, outlining specific actions and timelines. For example, "For the next two weeks, let's increase your outreach volume by 20% and focus on prospects in the healthcare sector."

Follow Up:
Check in frequently to track progress and adjust the plan if needed. Reinforce positive changes to build momentum.

Creating a Culture of Continuous Feedback
The best performance reviews don't feel like isolated events—they're part of an ongoing feedback loop. Foster a culture where:
- Reps feel comfortable asking for feedback anytime.
- Wins and lessons learned are shared openly.
- Regular check-ins are prioritized as opportunities to realign and grow.

Closing Thought
Performance reviews are more than a look back—they're a springboard for future success. By combining data, emotional insights, and collaborative goal-setting, you can transform reviews from a dreaded chore into a powerful tool for motivation and growth.

Chapter 10: Measuring Success

Using Feedback Loops for Continuous Improvement

Feedback loops are the secret sauce of high-performing BDR teams. They create a cycle of reflection, adjustment, and growth, ensuring your team isn't just working hard but working smarter. For leaders, feedback loops aren't about delivering critiques—they're about creating a culture where feedback flows freely and every insight becomes an opportunity for improvement.

Let's break down how to establish and optimize feedback loops that drive continuous improvement for both individuals and the team as a whole.

The Anatomy of a Feedback Loop
- **Observation:** Start by identifying what's happening. This could be a drop in response rates, a standout success in call conversions, or disengagement in meetings.
- **Feedback:** Provide actionable input based on your observations. Feedback should be clear, specific, and tied to outcomes.
- **Adjustment:** Collaborate with your team to implement changes, whether that's refining messaging, altering cadences, or addressing morale.
- **Re-Evaluation:** Measure the impact of those changes to determine what worked and what still needs improvement.

Building Effective Feedback Loops
Foster a Feedback-First Culture:
Encourage a mindset where feedback isn't feared but welcomed. Emphasize that feedback is about growth, not judgment. For instance, say, "Every insight we share makes us stronger as a team."

Leverage Multiple Sources:
Feedback should come from more than just you. Incorporate:
- Peer Feedback: Reps can share what they're learning or struggling with.
- Customer Feedback: Use replies, meeting notes, or prospect objections to refine outreach.
- Tool Analytics: Platforms like Gong or Outreach.io offer data-driven feedback on call effectiveness and cadence performance.

Keep Feedback Timely:
The closer feedback is to the action, the more impactful it will be. A call review loses its potency if delivered weeks later. Aim to provide feedback within a day or two of observing the behavior.

Make It Actionable:
Feedback should always answer, "What can I do differently?" Instead of saying, "Your email template isn't working," suggest, "Try adding a personalized subject line that references their recent funding announcement."

Feedback Loops for Individual Reps

Chapter 10: Measuring Success

Weekly 1:1 Check-Ins:
Use these sessions to discuss metrics, address challenges, and share insights. Frame questions to invite reflection, such as:
- "What's working well for you right now?"
- "What's been your biggest challenge this week?"

Role-Playing Scenarios:
Simulate prospecting calls or objection handling to identify areas for improvement. Offer immediate, constructive feedback and ask, "How do you think that went?"

Progress Tracking:
Create a simple feedback tracker for each rep, noting areas for improvement, agreed-upon actions, and outcomes. Revisit this tracker during follow-ups to highlight growth or recalibrate if needed.

Feedback Loops for the Team
Post-Mortem Reviews:
After major campaigns or quarters, analyze what went well and what didn't. Ask questions like:
- "What strategies drove the most success?"
- "What challenges could we have prepared for better?"

Peer Learning Sessions:
Hold monthly meetings where reps share their wins and insights. For example, a rep might present on a new objection-handling technique that increased their meeting acceptance rate.

Celebrate Iterations:
When a feedback-driven change leads to success, call it out. For instance, "Adjusting our cadence timing after last month's feedback led to a 15% increase in reply rates. Great work, team!"

Common Pitfalls to Avoid
Vague Feedback:
If feedback is too generic, it's hard to act on. Replace "Try harder to personalize your emails" with "Reference their recent job change in your email first line."

One-Way Communication:
Feedback isn't just top-down. Encourage reps to give feedback on strategies, tools, and your own leadership.

Feedback Overload:
Don't overwhelm reps with too many suggestions at once. Prioritize one or two actionable changes per feedback session.

Chapter 10: Measuring Success

Aligning Feedback Loops with Gen Z Expectations
For Gen Z reps, feedback is less about formal reviews and more about frequent, collaborative touchpoints. Here's how to tailor your approach:
- Incorporate Their Input: Ask, "What do you think is working well for you, and where could you use support?" This encourages self-reflection and buy-in.
- Keep It Real: Gen Z values authenticity. Be honest, transparent, and constructive without sugarcoating.
- Recognize Effort: Acknowledge progress, even if results aren't perfect. Say, "I can see you're experimenting with new call openings, and I appreciate your effort to adapt."

Closing the Feedback Loop
To close the loop, always follow up after providing feedback. Did the adjustment work? If yes, celebrate it. If not, revisit the strategy and try again. Continuous improvement isn't about getting it perfect on the first try—it's about learning, iterating, and growing as a team.

Key Takeaway
Feedback loops are the engine of growth for your team. By combining data-driven insights with collaborative, real-time coaching, you create a cycle where every interaction, success, or setback becomes a step toward greater performance.

Chapter 10: Measuring Success

Iterating on Strategies That Work

In the fast-paced world of BDR teams, success isn't a one-and-done event—it's a moving target. What works today might fall flat tomorrow, and the best leaders know how to stay ahead by constantly refining their strategies. Iteration isn't about reinventing the wheel; it's about tweaking and optimizing based on what's working, what's not, and what's changing in the market.

This section will explore how to identify successful strategies, iterate effectively, and scale what works without losing sight of the bigger picture.

The Iteration Mindset
To iterate successfully, leaders and teams need to:
- Embrace Experimentation: Every strategy is a hypothesis. Some will succeed, others won't—and that's okay.
- Stay Agile: Markets evolve, and so do buyers. Iteration is about staying flexible and adapting quickly.
- Be Data-Driven: Use metrics to guide decisions but remain open to insights from feedback and experience.

Identifying Strategies That Work
Before you iterate, you need to pinpoint what's worth iterating on. Start by analyzing:
- **High-Performing Metrics:** Look for standout performance in areas like response rates, show rates, or conversion ratios. For instance, if a particular cadence consistently outperforms others, it's worth investigating why.
- **Team Feedback:** Ask your reps what's resonating with prospects. The frontline often holds invaluable insights about what's working in real time.
- **Customer Signals:** Pay attention to buyer behavior, such as positive replies, meeting confirmations, or increased engagement with follow-up materials.

How to Iterate Effectively
- **Deconstruct Success:**
  When something works, don't just replicate it—understand it. For example:
    - If a certain email template drives a 20% reply rate, break it down: Is it the subject line, the tone, or the CTA that's driving engagement?
    - If calls to a specific industry outperform others, identify what's unique about that industry's pain points or decision-making process.
- **Test One Variable at a Time:**
  Avoid the temptation to overhaul everything at once. Instead, tweak a single element—such as the timing of follow-ups or the level of personalization in your emails—and measure the impact.
- **Involve the Team:**

Iteration is more effective when it's collaborative. Host brainstorming sessions to gather ideas and get buy-in from your reps. For example, say, "Our response rates in the finance vertical are lower than expected. What can we adjust in our

Chapter 10: Measuring Success

messaging to speak to their pain points more directly?"
- **Create a Feedback Loop:**
  After implementing a change, monitor its performance and gather input from the team. Ask:
  - "Did this feel easier or harder to execute?"
  - "What reactions are you getting from prospects?"
- **Scale Strategically:**
  When a strategy proves successful, roll it out to the broader team—but don't stop testing. Continue iterating at a smaller scale to keep improving.

Scaling What Works Without Diluting Impact

Scaling successful strategies is critical, but it requires a thoughtful approach to maintain their effectiveness:
- **Document Best Practices:** Turn effective tactics into playbook entries, complete with templates, examples, and step-by-step instructions.
- **Train the Team:** Host workshops or training sessions to ensure everyone understands and can execute the strategy consistently.
- **Monitor Quality:** As you scale, keep an eye on execution. For instance, if a highly personalized email template becomes overly templated, it may lose its impact.

Dealing with Strategies That Don't Work

Not every iteration will succeed, and that's part of the process. Here's how to handle strategies that fall short:
- **Analyze Without Blame:** Treat failures as learning opportunities. Ask, "What did we learn from this, and how can we apply it to future iterations?"
- **Course-Correct Quickly:** If a new cadence or messaging approach isn't yielding results, pivot promptly to avoid wasting time and resources.
- **Document Learnings:** Record failed strategies in your playbook with insights about why they didn't work. This can save time when testing future iterations.

Using Technology to Drive Iteration

Technology can supercharge your ability to test, measure, and refine strategies:
- **A/B Testing Tools:** Platforms like Outreach.io and SalesLoft allow you to test multiple versions of email cadences or call scripts.
- **Analytics Dashboards:** Use tools like Gong or HubSpot to track how changes impact key metrics, from call success rates to pipeline velocity.
- **Collaboration Tools:** Slack or Notion can help document and share insights in real time, keeping the team aligned on what's working.

Example Iterations in Action

Cadence Timing: If your original cadence includes follow-ups at Day 1, Day 3, and Day 5, test spreading them out to Days 2, 4, and 7 to see if it improves reply rates. Messaging Focus: Experiment with emphasizing ROI for executives versus product features for end-users to see which angle resonates more with your audience.

Iterating on Strategies That Work

Chapter 10: Measuring Success

Call Openers: Swap generic openers like "Is now a good time?" for tailored approaches like "I noticed your company just expanded into X market—how's that going?"

The Role of Gen Z in Iteration

Gen Z reps are natural collaborators and experimenters, making them valuable contributors to the iteration process:

- Embrace Their Creativity: Encourage reps to test new ideas and share what works. For instance, a Gen Z rep might suggest incorporating memes or pop culture references into LinkedIn outreach.
- Reward Experimentation: Celebrate not just successes but the effort to innovate. Say, "Your creative approach didn't yield results this time, but I love that you tried something new. Let's refine and try again."
- Foster Ownership: Involve them in building and refining playbooks. This deepens their engagement and ensures strategies reflect frontline realities.

Key Takeaways for Iteration

- Iteration is about progress, not perfection. Every tweak brings you closer to optimal performance.
- Keep the process agile, data-driven, and collaborative.
- Document and share learnings—both wins and losses—so the entire team grows together.

Chapter 11: Rethinking Frameworks

Common Qualification Frameworks: Why They're Outdated

Sales qualification frameworks have been the backbone of modern selling for decades. Created by forward-thinking sales leaders to bring structure and predictability to the chaotic world of prospecting, these frameworks were groundbreaking in their time. Each framework addressed specific challenges of its era, offering sales teams a repeatable way to evaluate opportunities and focus on high-value leads.

While these frameworks revolutionized sales when they were introduced, the complexities of today's buyer journeys have exposed their limitations. Let's explore what these frameworks are, why they worked, and why they're no longer enough.

What Are the Major Qualification Frameworks?

BANT (Budget, Authority, Need, Timeline)

- **What It Is:**
  One of the oldest and most widely known frameworks, BANT focuses on four key questions:
  - Budget: Does the prospect have the financial resources to buy?
  - Authority: Is this person the decision-maker?
  - Need: Does the prospect have a pain point your solution can solve?
  - Timeline: Is there urgency to implement the solution?

- **Why It Worked:**
  In an era where budgets were rigid, decision-making was centralized, and timelines were linear, BANT offered a simple, effective way to prioritize prospects. It streamlined conversations and ensured reps focused on deals likely to close.

- **Where It Falls Short Today:**
  Modern buyers often don't follow a clear timeline, and budgets are fluid. Authority is frequently distributed among multiple stakeholders, making it harder to pinpoint a single decision-maker. BANT also fails to account for the buyer's journey, motivations, or the cost of inaction.

CHAMP (Challenges, Authority, Money, Prioritization)

- **What It Is:**
  CHAMP is a more buyer-centric evolution of BANT, emphasizing the prospect's Challenges as the starting point. The framework evaluates:
  - Challenges: What problems are the prospect trying to solve?
  - Authority: Who has the power to approve the solution?
  - Money: Does the budget align with the solution's cost?
  - Prioritization: Where does this challenge sit among their other priorities?

- **Why It Worked:**
  By focusing on challenges first, CHAMP made the conversation less about qualification and more about problem-solving. It allowed reps to align solutions with real pain points, which was especially effective in mid-market sales.

Chapter 11: Rethinking Frameworks

- **Where It Falls Short Today:**
  CHAMP is still centered around a checklist-style approach that prioritizes the seller's need to qualify over the buyer's need to feel understood. It doesn't fully account for the complexities of multi-stakeholder decision-making or modern buyer behaviors.

MEDDIC (Metrics, Economic Buyer, Decision Criteria, Decision Process, Identify Pain, Champion)
- **What It Is:**
  MEDDIC is a data-heavy framework designed for enterprise sales. It focuses on metrics and measurable outcomes while identifying key players in the decision-making process. Its components are:
    - Metrics: Quantifiable benefits of the solution (e.g., ROI, cost savings).
    - Economic Buyer: The person with the authority to sign off on the deal.
    - Decision Criteria: The factors the buyer uses to evaluate solutions.
    - Decision Process: The steps the buyer takes to make a decision.
    - Identify Pain: The core problem driving the buyer's need for a solution.
    - Champion: An internal advocate pushing for your solution.
- **Why It Worked:**
  MEDDIC thrives in complex, high-stakes sales where measurable outcomes are critical. Its structured approach ensures reps navigate long sales cycles with precision.
- **Where It Falls Short Today:**
  MEDDIC can feel overly rigid and cumbersome for anything other than large enterprise deals. It also leans heavily on metrics and economic buyers, neglecting softer factors like internal politics, emotional drivers, or the growing influence of collaborative decision-making committees.

Why These Frameworks Worked in the Past
These frameworks were born out of necessity, designed to address specific challenges in sales:
- **BANT's Origin:** Developed by IBM in the 1960s, BANT emerged during a time when buyers relied on sellers as their primary source of information. The framework worked because it streamlined discovery and ensured reps focused on prospects with a clear ability and intent to buy.
- **CHAMP's Buyer Focus:** CHAMP arose as a response to the growing emphasis on solution-selling in the 1990s. By prioritizing challenges, it helped sellers engage buyers on a deeper level.
- **MEDDIC's Enterprise Expertise:** MEDDIC gained traction in the late 1990s at PTC, a software company, where it helped sales teams tackle complex, multi-stakeholder deals by adding structure and rigor.

Chapter 11: Rethinking Frameworks

Why They're Outdated Today
- **Buyer Behavior Has Changed:**
  Modern buyers don't want to feel "qualified." They want sellers who can empathize with their challenges, guide them through decision-making, and deliver value beyond a transaction.
- **Complexity Has Increased:**
  Most buying decisions now involve multiple stakeholders, each with unique priorities. Traditional frameworks often oversimplify this complexity.
- **Linear Journeys Are Rare:**
  Timelines, budgets, and even needs can shift throughout the buyer journey. Static frameworks can't adapt to these evolving dynamics.
- **Emotional Factors Matter:**
  Buying decisions aren't purely logical. Emotional factors like trust, perceived risk, and alignment with company culture play a huge role—and traditional frameworks overlook them entirely.

ANUM (Authority, Need, Urgency, Money)
- Focus: Similar to BANT but places greater emphasis on identifying the decision-maker early.
- Strength: Streamlines the process by prioritizing authority before other factors.
- Limitation: Overlooks deeper buyer motivations and doesn't adapt well to multi-stakeholder environments.

FAINT (Funds, Authority, Interest, Need, Timing)
- Focus: Prioritizes identifying interest over rigid budget qualifications.
- Strength: Works well in consultative selling where buyers may not have a pre-allocated budget.
- Limitation: Can lead to wasted effort on buyers with interest but no purchasing power.

GPCTBA (Goals, Plans, Challenges, Timeline, Budget, Authority)
- Focus: Designed for inbound sales by aligning buyer goals and plans with challenges and resources.
- Strength: Buyer-centric and helps build trust by emphasizing shared goals.
- Limitation: Can become too complex for quick qualification in fast-moving sales cycles.

SPIN (Situation, Problem, Implication, Need-Payoff)
- Focus: Uses open-ended questions to uncover the prospect's situation and implications of their challenges.
- Strength: Excellent for consultative selling, encouraging reps to explore deeper pain points.
- Limitation: Lacks structure for modern, data-driven qualification.

Chapter 11: Rethinking Frameworks

NEAT (Need, Economic Impact, Access to Authority, Timeline)
- Focus: Adds an emphasis on economic impact to the qualification process.
- Strength: Works well in deals where ROI is a critical factor.
- Limitation: May neglect emotional drivers and team-wide decision-making dynamics.

By understanding the limitations of these frameworks, we can see why qualification requires a fresh approach. This sets the stage for Introducing the IMPACT Framework for Qualification, which is purpose-built for today's dynamic, buyer-centric world.

Chapter 11: Rethinking Frameworks

Introducing the IMPACT Framework for Qualification

The sales world is evolving rapidly, and traditional frameworks often feel too rigid and transactional to meet today's challenges. Buyers are more informed, decision-making is more collaborative, and priorities shift in real-time. This is why the IMPACT Framework exists: a modern, dynamic approach to qualification that blends structure with flexibility, empathy, and strategic thinking.

IMPACT redefines qualification, focusing on collaboration and partnership rather than just checking boxes. It aligns with the complexities of the current and future sales ecosystem, where success hinges on understanding, co-creating, and building trust with buyers.

What Makes IMPACT Different?

1. **Future-Focused:** Built for the evolving buyer journey, it adapts to fluid timelines, collaborative decision-making, and emotional drivers.
2. **Buyer-Centric:** Prioritizes understanding the buyer's world over the seller's checklist, fostering deeper trust and alignment.
3. **Strategic Over Transactional:** Goes beyond qualifying leads to building partnerships and influencing outcomes.
4. **Collaborative at Its Core:** Recognizes that today's sales cycles involve multiple stakeholders and values collective buy-in over individual authority.

The Components of IMPACT

Each letter in IMPACT represents a crucial step in the qualification process, designed to uncover insights, align goals, and drive forward momentum.

I: Identifying Pain Points

Understanding the buyer's pain is at the heart of any sales conversation. But with IMPACT, it's not just about surface-level pain—it's about digging deep into both logical and emotional challenges.

- **What It Covers:**
    - Operational inefficiencies.
    - Strategic misalignments.
    - Emotional pain (stress, frustration, missed opportunities).
- **How to Approach It:**
    Ask open-ended questions that encourage the buyer to share their challenges. For example:
    - "What's the biggest roadblock keeping your team from achieving its goals?"
    - "How is this challenge impacting your team's morale or efficiency?"
- **Key Outcome:**
    A clear understanding of both the problem and the buyer's emotional connection to solving it, creating the foundation for urgency.

Chapter 11: Rethinking Frameworks

M: Measuring the Cost of Inaction
Often, buyers don't move forward because they don't fully understand the consequences of maintaining the status quo. IMPACT emphasizes helping buyers quantify the cost of doing nothing.
- **What It Covers:**
    - Financial costs (revenue loss, operational inefficiency).
    - Strategic risks (falling behind competitors, missing opportunities).
    - Human costs (burnout, disengagement).
- **How to Approach It:**
  Use probing questions to highlight the implications of inaction. For example:
    - "If this problem persists for the next 6 months, what does that look like for your team?"
    - "What opportunities might you miss if this issue remains unresolved?"
- **Key Outcome:**
  The buyer understands the urgency of solving their problem, creating momentum toward action.

P: Prioritizing Leadership Buy-In
Today's buying decisions rarely rest with one person. IMPACT recognizes the importance of engaging leaders early and aligning with their priorities.
- **What It Covers:**
    - Identifying champions and influencers.
    - Mapping organizational priorities.
    - Engaging leadership in meaningful ways.
- **How to Approach It:**
  Focus on understanding leadership dynamics and their strategic goals. Questions like these help:
    - "Who would benefit most from solving this challenge?"
    - "What outcomes are most important to leadership when evaluating solutions?"
- **Key Outcome:**
  Early leadership buy-in ensures alignment across the organization and streamlines decision-making.

A: Assessing Readiness
Qualification isn't just about interest—it's about timing and alignment. IMPACT includes a readiness assessment to gauge whether the buyer is prepared to act.
- **What It Covers:**
    - Internal alignment and bandwidth.
    - Budget and resource availability.
    - Timeline feasibility.
- **How to Approach It:**
  Ask questions that uncover the buyer's readiness to commit. For example:
    - "What steps have you taken so far to address this issue?"
    - "What would need to happen internally for this to move forward?"

IMPACT Framework for Qualification

Chapter 11: Rethinking Frameworks

- **Key Outcome:**
  A realistic understanding of the buyer's stage in their journey, allowing for tailored next steps.

C: Collaborating on Solutions

Gone are the days of pitching solutions in a vacuum. IMPACT emphasizes co-creating a vision for success with the buyer.

- **What It Covers:**
  - Building trust through collaboration.
  - Aligning solutions with the buyer's vision.
  - Creating ownership for the buyer in the proposed solution.
- **How to Approach It:**
  Use the buyer's input to craft a solution that resonates with their needs. Questions like these help:
  - "What would an ideal outcome look like for you?"
  - "How can we adapt this solution to fit your unique situation?"
- **Key Outcome:**
  A buyer who feels invested in the solution and confident in its ability to address their challenges.

T: Tracking Stakeholder Engagement

IMPACT doesn't stop at identifying stakeholders—it emphasizes continuous engagement to ensure alignment and momentum.

- **What It Covers:**
  - Mapping all decision-makers and influencers.
  - Monitoring engagement levels throughout the sales cycle.
  - Addressing concerns proactively.
- **How to Approach It:**
  Stay proactive with questions like:
  - "Who else would need to weigh in on this decision?"
  - "What concerns might other stakeholders have about moving forward?"
- **Key Outcome:**
  A comprehensive view of stakeholder involvement, minimizing the risk of last-minute objections.

Why IMPACT Works for the Current and Future Sales Ecosystem

- **Adaptable:** Fits both transactional and enterprise sales, adapting to different levels of complexity.
- **Human-Centric:** Recognizes the emotional, strategic, and collaborative aspects of modern buying decisions.
- **Scalable:** Can be implemented across teams and tailored to unique industries or sales cycles.

IMPACT is the framework for sales leaders who are ready to leave outdated methods behind and embrace the future of qualification.

Chapter 11: Rethinking Frameworks

Limitations of the IMPACT Framework

While the IMPACT Framework is designed to address the complexities of modern sales, like any methodology, it's not without its limitations. Acknowledging these helps leaders implement the framework effectively and adapt it to their specific contexts.

Requires Skilled Reps with Consultative Selling Expertise

IMPACT shifts qualification from a transactional approach to a consultative one. While this is one of its greatest strengths, it also means that not every rep will excel with this framework right away.

- Challenge: New or less-experienced reps may struggle to ask open-ended questions, handle nuanced buyer conversations, or navigate emotional and strategic dynamics effectively.
- How to Address It:
    - Invest in training on consultative selling and active listening.
    - Role-play IMPACT scenarios regularly to build confidence and fluency.
    - Pair less-experienced reps with mentors or team leads who excel at consultative conversations.

Time-Intensive for High-Velocity Sales Cycles

IMPACT is inherently thorough, focusing on deep buyer understanding and stakeholder engagement. This level of depth can feel cumbersome in high-velocity sales environments with short cycles and transactional deals.

- Challenge: Reps may find it difficult to implement all components of the framework when they need to qualify dozens of leads daily.
- How to Address It:
    - Streamline the framework for specific scenarios. For example, focus on Identifying Pain Points, Assessing Readiness, and Collaborating on Solutions for high-velocity deals while saving the full framework for enterprise opportunities.
    - Leverage automation to handle repetitive tasks, like tracking engagement or monitoring readiness signals in your CRM.

Complexity in Multi-Stakeholder Environments

While IMPACT emphasizes tracking stakeholder engagement, managing multiple stakeholders can still become overwhelming, especially in large enterprises with opaque decision-making structures.

- Challenge: Identifying, engaging, and aligning multiple stakeholders requires a significant amount of time, research, and persistence.
- How to Address It:
    - Use tools like Gong, ZoomInfo, or LinkedIn Sales Navigator to map organizational structures and identify potential stakeholders.
    - Document all stakeholder interactions in your CRM to ensure nothing slips through the cracks.
    - Lean on champions in the buyer's org to help navigate internal dynamics.

Chapter 11: Rethinking Frameworks

Potential for Misalignment with Strict Metrics-Driven Leadership
IMPACT focuses heavily on collaboration, buyer-centricity, and emotional factors, which may feel intangible to sales leaders who prioritize hard metrics like activity volume or quota attainment.
- Challenge: Teams working under traditional leadership may find it difficult to balance IMPACT's qualitative approach with quantitative expectations.
- How to Address It:
    - Align IMPACT metrics with organizational goals. For example, track leading indicators such as the number of pain points identified or stakeholders engaged.
    - Present IMPACT results as a combination of both qualitative (e.g., improved stakeholder alignment) and quantitative (e.g., increased win rates) outcomes.

Relies on the Buyer's Willingness to Engage
IMPACT requires buyers to actively participate in collaborative conversations. If buyers are disengaged, unavailable, or unwilling to share insights, it can be challenging to implement the framework effectively.
- Challenge: Some buyers may not be forthcoming about their pain points or internal dynamics, especially early in the sales process.
- How to Address It:
    - Build trust early by focusing on small wins and demonstrating value before diving into deeper qualification.
    - Use discovery calls to highlight your expertise and ask questions that encourage buyers to open up.
    - Leverage external research to fill gaps, such as identifying pain points or understanding readiness based on industry trends.

Difficulty Scaling Across Diverse Teams
IMPACT's flexibility makes it powerful, but it also introduces variability. Reps may interpret and execute the framework differently, leading to inconsistent results across teams.
- Challenge: Without proper implementation, the framework can lose its effectiveness if team members use it inconsistently.
- How to Address It:
    - Develop a standardized playbook that outlines specific questions, examples, and metrics for each component of IMPACT.
    - Monitor adoption through regular coaching sessions and deal reviews.
    - Use role-playing to standardize execution and identify areas for improvement.

Results May Take Time to Materialize
Because IMPACT is a relationship-driven and consultative framework, it may take longer to see tangible results compared to transactional frameworks like BANT or CHAMP.

Chapter 11: Rethinking Frameworks

- Challenge: Teams under pressure to hit short-term targets may feel frustrated by the longer ramp-up time for results.
- How to Address It:
    - Communicate realistic expectations during the implementation phase.
    - Highlight incremental wins, such as higher-quality conversations or increased stakeholder engagement, even if deals take longer to close.
    - Pair IMPACT with tools that track early indicators of success, like improved buyer responsiveness or higher pipeline velocity.

Acknowledging the Trade-Offs
No framework is perfect, and IMPACT's depth and adaptability come with trade-offs. However, these limitations are surmountable with proper implementation, training, and support. By embracing its strengths while mitigating its challenges, leaders can unlock IMPACT's full potential to drive smarter, more strategic sales outcomes.

Chapter 11: Rethinking Frameworks

How IMPACT Makes Qualification Smarter and More Effective

The IMPACT Framework isn't just a tweak to existing qualification methods—it's a fundamental shift in how sales teams engage with prospects. Designed for the complexities of today's buyer journeys, IMPACT focuses on collaboration, empathy, and actionable insights to drive better outcomes. By addressing the limitations of traditional frameworks and aligning with the needs of modern buyers, IMPACT ensures smarter qualification and sustained success.

Aligning Qualification with Buyer Behavior

Traditional frameworks often treat qualification as a one-sided exercise, focusing on the seller's need to disqualify leads quickly. IMPACT flips this script by prioritizing the buyer's journey.

- Why It Works:
  - Buyers today demand deeper understanding and partnership. IMPACT creates space for reps to explore the buyer's challenges, motivations, and decision-making dynamics.
- Key Differentiator:
  - IMPACT doesn't assume a linear path or fixed criteria. Instead, it adapts to the buyer's priorities, making it more effective for navigating real scenarios.

Creating Urgency Without Pressure

One of the standout features of IMPACT is its focus on the Cost of Inaction (COI). Instead of relying on arbitrary timelines or external deadlines, it helps buyers understand the tangible and intangible risks of maintaining the status quo.

- How It's Different:
  - Traditional frameworks often emphasize timelines, which can feel forced or irrelevant to the buyer. IMPACT shifts the conversation to what the buyer stands to lose by not acting.
- Example:
  - A rep might say, "If this inefficiency persists, what impact could that have on your team's morale or ability to hit growth targets this year?" This approach feels consultative rather than pushy, encouraging the buyer to self-identify urgency.

Addressing Multi-Stakeholder Dynamics

With an average of 6-10 stakeholders involved in most buying decisions, single-contact qualification frameworks fall short. IMPACT incorporates stakeholder mapping and tracking, ensuring alignment across the entire decision-making team.

- Why It Works:
  - It proactively engages all influencers and decision-makers, reducing the risk of last-minute objections or internal misalignment.
- Key Feature:
  - The Tracking Stakeholder Engagement component encourages reps to ask

Chapter 11: Rethinking Frameworks

questions like, "Who else would need to be on board for this to succeed?" and to continuously monitor engagement levels throughout the deal.

Making Qualification Collaborative
IMPACT recognizes that buyers are more likely to engage when they feel ownership of the solution. Instead of pitching a ready-made answer, it emphasizes co-creating the roadmap to success.
- Why It Works:
  - Collaboration builds trust, strengthens relationships, and increases the buyer's confidence in your solution.
- Key Feature:
  - The Collaborating on Solutions step ensures that the buyer's voice is central to the process, fostering alignment and buy-in.

Balancing Emotional and Data-Driven Insights
IMPACT goes beyond numbers by addressing the emotional factors that influence decisions, such as trust, risk aversion, and internal politics. By blending emotional indicators with hard data, it creates a more holistic qualification process.
- Why It Works:
  - Decisions are rarely based on logic alone. A framework that incorporates emotional intelligence resonates more deeply with buyers.
- Key Example:
  - During the Identifying Pain Points step, a rep might ask, "How is this issue impacting your team's morale or confidence?" This uncovers motivations that traditional frameworks overlook.

Driving Long-Term Value
Qualification isn't just about closing deals—it's about creating lasting partnerships. IMPACT ensures that deals are built on shared goals and aligned expectations, increasing the likelihood of customer success and retention.
- How It's Different:
  - Traditional frameworks often focus on short-term wins, while IMPACT prioritizes long-term relationships by building trust and delivering measurable value.
- Key Outcome:
  - Buyers who feel supported during the sales process are more likely to stay loyal and become advocates for your solution.

How IMPACT Adapts to Different Sales Environments
IMPACT's versatility allows it to excel across various scenarios:
- Transactional Sales: Focus on core elements like Identifying Pain Points and Assessing Readiness to qualify leads quickly without sacrificing depth
- Enterprise Sales: Use the full framework to navigate complex decision-making, emphasizing Stakeholder Engagement and Collaborating on Solutions to align diverse priorities.

IMPACT is Smarter and More Effective

Chapter 11: Rethinking Frameworks

- Inbound Sales: Adapt IMPACT to guide prospects who have already expressed interest, focusing on Cost of Inaction and Readiness to accelerate their journey.

Measurable Results with IMPACT
Implementing IMPACT not only improves qualification but also drives better outcomes across key metrics:
- Higher Win Rates: By addressing pain points deeply and collaboratively, deals are more likely to close.
- Faster Sales Cycles: Helping buyers understand the cost of inaction accelerates decision-making.
- Increased Stakeholder Alignment: Proactively engaging all influencers minimizes late-stage surprises.
- Greater Buyer Satisfaction: The collaborative approach fosters trust and ensures solutions are tailored to buyer needs.

Why IMPACT Is Built for the Future of Sales
The sales landscape will continue to evolve, with buyers demanding even greater personalization, flexibility, and value. IMPACT is designed to grow with these trends, making it a framework that's not just relevant for today but essential for tomorrow.

Chapter : Close

Closing Thoughts: From Controlled Chaos to Unstoppable IMPACT
Congratulations—you've made it to the end of this book without skipping to the last chapter. (Or maybe you did, in which case, shame on you. Go back and read the rest. I'll wait.) Whether you devoured every page or skimmed like a caffeinated speed reader, you're now armed with everything you need to lead a BDR team that crushes it—and has a little fun along the way.

A Toast to the Chaos
Let's be real: leading a BDR team is like playing whack-a-mole at a carnival, but the moles are leads, and the carnival is on fire. You've got quotas breathing down your neck, a team full of creative chaos agents (we love them), and prospects who ghost like it's their full-time job. Yet, here you are, not just surviving but thriving.

You're not just juggling flaming chainsaws—you're building something extraordinary:
- A team that's rewriting what success looks like (and occasionally what professionalism looks like).
- A culture that says, "Yes, we'll book that meeting, but we're going to have some laughs along the way."
- A legacy of leadership that proves you don't need to be a rockstar to shine.

If that's not worth a celebratory dance in your office chair, I don't know what is.

The Rules of the Game
Before you go leading your team into battle (or just another team huddle), let's recap some survival tips we've covered:

1. It's Not About You: A great leader is like a great bartender—you make everyone else look good while quietly solving their problems.
2. Celebrate the Wins (and Laugh at the Fails): Whether it's landing a massive account or realizing that your "clever" subject line got flagged as spam, every experience is a step forward. (Also, maybe run subject lines past someone next time.)
3. Stay Weird: Sales is stressful enough. Inject humor, embrace your quirks, and remember: A team that laughs together sells together.
4. Iterate Relentlessly: No one gets it right the first time, not even Beyoncé. Keep tweaking, improving, and finding new ways to IMPACT.

A Challenge for You
You didn't think I'd let you off the hook without homework, did you? Here's your final challenge:

- Do One Thing Today: Pick something from this book and put it into action. Maybe it's redesigning your qualification framework. Maybe it's starting a Slack channel for the best prospect excuses your team has heard this week (we all need a laugh). Whatever it is, just start.

Chapter : Close

- Ask for Feedback: Pro tip: "How am I doing as your leader?" works better when paired with pizza or donuts. Bravery tastes better with snacks.
- Celebrate Something Dumb: Did someone send an email with a typo that landed a reply anyway? Give them an award for "Most Persuasive Typo." Teams that laugh together stay together.

What's Next?
Now that you're armed with a better playbook than most action movie villains, here's what I hope for you:
- That your team meetings feel less like PowerPoint purgatory and more like strategy sessions with bonus snacks.
- That your pipeline is so robust it makes your CRM blush.
- That your leadership legacy includes both hitting numbers and hitting a few karaoke nights with your team.

Above all, I hope you lead with curiosity, adapt with courage, and never lose sight of the fact that sales is as much about people as it is about metrics.

Go Be Legendary
So, what now? Now, you go make IMPACT. You go lead your team with humor, resilience, and just the right amount of sarcasm. You go prove that leadership doesn't have to be flashy to be unforgettable.

This isn't goodbye—it's, "Go get 'em, champ." It's, "Don't forget to tell your team that joke about the CRM." It's, "I hope you send me a postcard from the top because that's where you're headed."

With all the wit, wisdom, and caffeine it took to write this,
Your Co-Author along with GPT

P.S. If anyone asks, yes, we totally meant for that typo on page 42 to be there. It's symbolic. ●

www.ingramcontent.com/pod-product-compliance
Lightning Source LLC
Chambersburg PA
CBHW071027240526
45469CB00006BD/2121